ARTILLERY SCOUT

ARTILLERY SCOUT

The Story of a Forward Observer
with the U.S. Field Artillery
in World War I

JAMES G. BILDER

CASEMATE
Philadelphia & Oxford

Published in the United States of America and Great Britain in 2014 by
CASEMATE PUBLISHERS
908 Darby Road, Havertown, PA 19083
and
10 Hythe Bridge Street, Oxford, OX1 2EW

ISBN 978-1-61200-271-2
Digital Edition: ISBN 978-1-61200-272-9

Cataloging-in-publication data is available from the Library of Congress and
the British Library.

10 9 8 7 6 5 4 3 2 1

Printed and bound in the United States of America.

For a complete list of Casemate titles please contact:

CASEMATE PUBLISHERS (US)
Telephone (610) 853-9131, Fax (610) 853-9146
E-mail: casemate@casematepublishing.com

CASEMATE PUBLISHERS (UK)
Telephone (01865) 241249, Fax (01865) 794449
E-mail: casemate-uk@casematepublishing.co.uk

Photo on title page:
An American gun crew operating a French 75mm in combat. The American Army had
very few of its own artillery pieces in France and requisitioned roughly 4,000 artillery
pieces from the French. The fact that the gun is being fired on open ground as opposed
to being in a casemate is a testament to the rapid mobility of the American and Allied
forces in the autumn of 1918.—*Courtesy of First Division Museum*

MIX
Paper from
responsible sources
FSC
www.fsc.org   FSC® C011935

Contents

*To the memory of my Grandfather, Leonard F. Fairfield,
and all those who were a part of America's Lost Generation.
Also, to my son, James M. Bilder, and his comrades in arms who
continue the proud tradition of Illinois' 33rd Infantry Brigade.*

CADENCE OF THE U.S. ARMY FIELD ARTILLERY

Over hill, over dale, we have hit the dusty trail,
and those caissons go rolling along.
"Counter march! Right about!"
hear those wagon soldiers shout,
while those caissons go rolling along.

For it's "Hi! Hi! Hee!" in the Field Artillery,
Call off your numbers loud and strong.
And where e'er we go you will always know
that those caissons go rolling along.

To the front, day and night where the doughboys dig and fight
and those caissons go rolling along.
Our barrage will be fired on the rockets flare
while those caissons go rolling along.

For it's "Hi! Hi! Hee!" in the Field Artillery,
Call off your numbers loud and strong.
And where e'er we go you will always
know that those caissons go rolling along.

With the cav'lry, boot to boot we will join in the pursuit
and those caissons go rolling along.
Action front, at a trot, volley fire with shell and shot
while those caissons go rolling along.

For it's "Hi! Hi! Hee!" in the Field Artillery,
Call off your numbers loud and strong.
And where e'er we go you will always know
that those caissons go rolling along.

Should the foe penetrate, ev'ry gunner lies in wait
and those caissons go rolling along.

Fire at will, lay 'em low, never stop for any foe
while those caissons go rolling along.

For it's "Hi! Hi! Hee!" in the Field Artillery,
Call off your numbers loud and strong.
And where e'er we go you will always know
that those caissons go rolling along.

But if fate me should call, and in action I should fall
keep those caissons go rolling along.
Then in peace I'll abide when I take my final ride
on a caisson that's rolling along.

American artillery crew in a casemate crowded around their French 75mm field gun for a picture. The French 75 ("Soixante-Quinze") was the standard artillery piece used by the AEF. It had a crew of six men who were cross trained but could still function effectively with as few as three. The secrets of the 75's effectiveness were so closely guarded by the French that even their American allies did not know everything about the gun.—Courtesy of First Division Museum

Foreword

T O MOST AMERICANS, World War I—AKA the "Great War"—
is not even a dim memory; it has passed into ancient history.
Some schools and textbooks don't even mention it.

And yet, this massive conflict that cost almost nine million human lives and was, until the next global conflict that followed less than a generation later, the greatest man-made disaster the world had ever seen. Because it was so terrible, it is no wonder that so many people believed that it was "the war to end all wars." After all, who could possibly engage in another war if the final butcher's bill was so ghastly?

Although the United States did not officially enter the war until April 1917 when Congress declared war on Germany and the Central Powers, and its first troops did not reach French soil until June 1917, America still lost 116,000 troops in just seventeen months—double what the U.S lost during the entire ten years of the Vietnam War. Many of the other warring nations lost far, far more.

As the eminent British historian Sir Martin Gilbert noted, World War I "changed our world. In its wake, empires toppled, monarchies fell, whole political systems realigned. Instabilities became institutionalized, enmities enshrined. Revolution swept to power ideologies of the left and right. And the social order shifted seismically. Manners, mores, codes of behavior; literature and the arts; education and class distinctions: all underwent a vast sea change."

One of the problems with writing about such a massive, history-alter-

9

ing event as World War I is that it is too big, too massive, to wrap our heads around. The statistics numb and overwhelm us and dredge up feelings of disbelief. Who can truly grasp the idea of nine million deaths? Or, for that matter, the fifty million in the war that followed?

By concentrating primarily on one individual—his grandfather, Leonard ("Len") Fairfield—James Bilder helps us comprehend the personal impact of this event. He focuses tightly on the few, rather than using a wide-angle lens to view the many. Len Fairfield, whom the reader will soon discover, served as a young "Yank" artilleryman from Chicago in the Illinois National Guard's 58th Field Artillery Brigade that supported the 1st and 89th Divisions. (Bilder also doesn't neglect his grandmother, Maggie, who kept the home fires burning.)

Until now, most accounts of WWI have concentrated on the trench-bound mud rats of the infantry, and the fledgling aerial corps with their gallant "knights of the air" doing battle in their flimsy "aeroplanes." Bilder's book is the first in recent memory to be devoted almost entirely to the life of a footman serving the "King of Battle"—the artillery. And, if nothing else, World War I is remembered for its prolific use of artillery.

From small, ordinary field guns (such as the famous French 75) to guns so huge they had to be mounted and transported on several railroad cars, artillery dominated the battlefield, churning the farm fields, over which the war was fought, into bottomless bogs, and blasting soldiers into tiny, bloody scraps of meat. Many of those who survived the barrages were never the same mentally, coming down with a condition called "shell shock," later re-termed post-traumatic stress disorder, or PTSD.

Bilder expertly captures the mundane military details, such as Army doctors shoving blunt inoculation needles into the arms of recruits, the tedium of seemingly endless close-order drill, rudimentary marksmanship, horsemanship, and learning to correctly put on gas masks—even on the horses. He introduces us to Len's beloved French horse, Annabel. He takes us to Len's artillery training at Camp Le Valdahon, France, and thrusts us into the titanic battles in the St. Mihiel and Meuse-Argonne sectors.

Fairfield was involved up to his knees in the mud, blood, and mustard gas of the Meuse-Argonne Offensive that started in late September 1918, involved 1.2 million American soldiers, continued for 47 brutal days, and cost the lives of 26,000 Yanks—the bloodiest single battle in American history.

Once the war was finally and truly over, and his unit was occupying Luxembourg, Fairfield was admitted to a military hospital—not for any physical or psychological wounds, but for nearly fatal cases of flu and pneumonia. Weak and emaciated, he celebrated victory quietly, without visible joy or fanfare. And, somehow, his horse Annabel survived the war, too, but she had to be left behind. Fairfield's return to Chicago resulted in him and Maggie becoming parents to ten children, including the author's mother.

Using his grandfather's letters and other family archives, Bilder has done a masterful job of describing in exacting detail the life of the typical American "Doughboy" of World War I.

Everyone who fought in that awful meat grinder is now gone. But, thanks to authors like James Bilder, their courage and sacrifice has been preserved in time capsules like this one—a piece of amber in which is encased a piece of human history that must never be allowed to be forgotten. Far too high a price was paid for it.

Flint Whitlock
Military historian

A battery commander instructs an artillery crew in training. American infantry often received woefully inadequate training but their artillery units were trained extensively not only in the states but in France as well.—Courtesy of Illinois National Guard

Artillery rounds ranging from high explosives to gas shells were carried in caissons. Field guns were limbered to caissons and both drawn by horse or mule teams.—Courtesy of Illinois National Guard

Introduction

I NEVER KNEW EITHER of my grandfathers. My dad's father died at age 26 in December of 1918, a victim of the Great Flu Pandemic. That was five months before my dad was even born. My mom's dad, on the other hand, lived to be 69 but I was only three-and-a-half years old when he succumbed to pneumonia in early 1962 during end-stage throat cancer.

Both men were mysteries to me, and when I entered my teens I began to inquire about them. My dad's father, Michael, did not really live long enough to establish much of a legacy. He was an ethnic German living with his parents and siblings in a largely German settlement called Jaksic in Croatia.

A skilled barrel maker (cooper) with a fifth grade education, it appears he came through Ellis Island in January of 1912 using the old country spelling of his surname (in German "P" can often be used in place of "B" thus turning "Bilder" into "Pilder"). It looks as though he also used his father's first name (Joseph) and place of birth (Kislod, Hungary) to avoid the Austrian-Hungarian draft and the Great War that was looming large on the European horizon. He came to the German neighborhoods on the Southside of Chicago where he met and then married my grandmother in July of 1917.

He applied his trade at a small brewery near his home while they lived in a cold water flat on South Wells Street. They were active in St. George Parish, my grandfather was a member of the fraternal Woodmen of the

Comma Splice

13

World (Wentworth Camp 298), loved to dance, play cards, and was a very popular guy. They had a premature stillborn son (Joseph) in June of 1918 and my dad was conceived about three months later. 1918 closed with my paternal grandfather's burial. End of story! At least his, but he did father my dad who had a distinguished record as a rifleman in Patton's Third Army, but then that's another book altogether (literally).

My mom's dad is a different matter entirely and, in fact, another book. Like my own father, my maternal grandfather was born and raised on Chicago's Southside. He too, knew rough neighborhoods, real poverty, and an unhappy home life, yet still possessed a fierce determination to make something of himself.

The similarity between my dad's experiences in and around World War II and his future father-in-law's in World War I are uncanny. Both men fell in love as their country fell into war, both were drafted into the army, and both lost friends as they engaged in bloody close quarter combat in France. Fortunately for me, both men returned safely to civilian life and their respective sweethearts who had waited faithfully for their homecoming. Both men were prolific and raised large families. It was my mother's dad, Len Fairfield, who reluctantly went forward to play his miniscule role in the most catastrophic war that humanity had waged upon itself up to that time—the "Great War."

Even a hundred years after the fact, the First World War still gnaws at us like a wound that won't heal. It seems to epitomize the futility of war when we look at the actual spark that ignited the conflict, the tactics used to slaughter millions over static battlefields, and the seemingly futile treaty written at Versailles. It mocks the idea of winning peace through war (the "war to end all wars"), and its possible avoidance calls longingly to mind John Greenleaf Whittier's quote, "of all the words of tongue or pen, the saddest are these, 'it might have been.'"

Unlike their sons who fought World War II and became known as the "Greatest Generation," the American "Doughboys" who fought in World War I have forever been enshrined in history as the "Lost Generation." Like the war itself, they symbolize all the hopes and dreams washed away in the rivers of blood—all the promise that was lost to the world.

The reasons for the conflict and why America eventually entered it have been written about in countless volumes. It seems there is precious little left to be revealed about those aspects of the war.

Even the American Army that fought in it, the American Expeditionary Force (AEF), has been closely scrutinized and reviewed. Its lack of preparation at the outset of war, its dependence on its European allies for weapons, equipment, and training have been well documented in fascinating detail. But, the larger, or perhaps smaller but equally compelling, question still remains. What was the entire event like for the average American soldier who took part in it?

The term "Doughboy" once meant more than a cute, talking, bakeable character that giggles when poked in the tummy by a giant finger. During America's involvement in WWI, and for a considerable time thereafter, "Doughboys" epitomized military courage, grit, and all that was to be admired in a soldier or marine.

The individual Doughboy was like his entire army. He had to be created. He had to be inducted, clothed, fed, trained, equipped, and readied in every way for the task that lay before him. What was that experience all about for the typical American soldier of that day?

He was going up against an enemy that had been schooled in war for almost four years and whose performance on the battlefield was unequaled. The Germans had destroyed the Serbian Army in 1915, the Rumanian Army in 1916, the Italian Army in 1917, and forced the Russians out of the war in 1918. What could the Americans possibly do against such a foe? And yet, despite the seemingly certain logic that the Americans could never be made ready to intervene effectively before German submarines forced Britain into starvation and German armies crushed France into submission, the American Doughboys provided the necessary impetus to turn the war in the Allies' favor and secure victory over Germany and her allies.

How was this done, especially when many Doughboys did not believe, or at least doubted, the very validity of their country being a belligerent in a European conflict? This book seeks to provide some needed insight into that question. It deals not with the larger questions of governments, generals, or armies, but rather the view from a single individual who, like his own nation, was reluctantly drawn into the conflict and forced to live with its consequences both during and after the war. It provides a clear perspective of precisely who and what the typical American Doughboy was all about.

It is interesting to note that my grandfather was not, unlike the vast majority of Doughboys, in the infantry. He was an Artillery Scout, or what has been known since World War II as a Forward Observer. He was a firsthand witness to the carnage, and it was artillery after all that accounted for the vast majority of that carnage, producing roughly seventy percent of the war's casualties.

I was blessed to have my father around so that we could produce a first-hand account of his WWII experiences as a rifleman with Patton. I did not have that luxury when writing about my grandfather's experiences. Fortunately, my grandfather shared his combat experiences with my dad and he passed those on to me—usually when we were working on his WWII accounts. My grandfather had spoken freely about his non-combat military experiences with everyone, and both my parents and my grandmother had told me all about them.

The irony of fate cannot be missed when one contemplates the fact that my paternal grandfather successfully avoided military service with the Central Powers in World War I and died of disease living in the safety of civilian life just one month after the Armistice. My maternal grandfather, on the other hand, served in the U.S. Army and survived combat, including the single most deadly battle in American history (the Argonne), as well as flu and pneumonia, and lived to return to civilian life and grow old. It brings to mind a quote from General Joshua Chamberlain, a Medal of Honor recipient in the American Civil War, "there is no promise of life in peace and no decree of death in war."

This work could in some ways be considered a prequel to *A Foot Soldier for Patton,* with the obvious difference being that I had to make this work a third person rather than a first person account. Most of the dialogue I based on my grandfather's personality traits, though a reasonable number of quotes are precise and they will likely be obvious to the reader due to the events surrounding them.

The extensive details in the military records of the 33rd Infantry Division and the diaries of some its officers have made many circumstances available, right down to weather and road conditions, and this was an

Sources

enormous aid to my efforts. It enabled me to determine precisely where and when some of my grandfather's experiences occurred.

This work will by no means provide all one wants to know about the American Doughboys of WWI. It does, however, provide a necessary and often neglected view of such momentous events from the ground, or in this case shell hole, on up. Hopefully, it records for history some of the courage and sacrifice of truly extraordinary men and will help any reader to find at least a part of the Lost Generation.

shades of Thucydides?

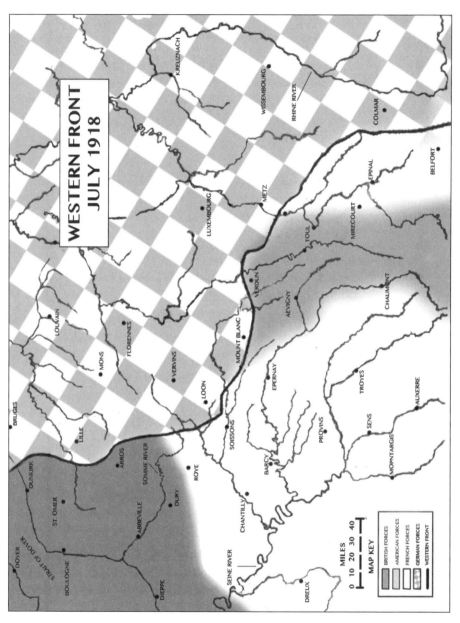

WESTERN FRONT
JULY 1918

MAP KEY
MILES
0 10 20 30 40
BRITISH FORCES
AMERICAN FORCES
FRENCH FORCES
GERMAN FORCES
WESTERN FRONT

this map is not helpful

. . . .

CHAPTER I

Neutral Land, a Common Man, the Makings of Love and War

W HEN THE "GREAT WAR" first erupted in August of 1914, virtually every American was happy that the United States had no part in it. Since the height of the Roman Empire, nearly two thousand years earlier, the European continent seemed to be continually awash in conflict. Europe seemed to Americans to be a place of never ending wars and conquests. Provinces and peoples bounced back and forth between nations like tennis balls in hotly contested matches.

Americans felt that Europeans experienced peace in only brief spurts, lasting long enough to draw up fresh maps designating the spoils of war in the form of changes in national boundaries and territories. This was then followed by new wars that would erupt before the ink on the peace treaties and maps had time enough to dry. This cycle seemed to repeat itself with almost as much regularity and certainty as the change of seasons.

Now, in the twentieth century, a perceived time of heightened reason and enlightenment, the Europeans were at war with each other yet again. This time, no less, over the assassination of an Archduke and his wife by a crazed nationalist! The Europeans appeared to Americans to look for excuses to fight one another.

This current conflict did not seem to bear any more relevance to Americans than the countless ones that preceded it. Europeans would be killing each other infinitum, and if that was their wish then America could best serve its own interests by staying far removed and uninvolved. After all, this was the very thing that America's first President, George Washington, had envisioned and warned against when making his farewell address as he urged his fellow countrymen to avoid "entangling alliances."

War in Europe may have erupted in 1914, but Americans in 1914 were limiting their struggles to domestic politics. Progressives, socialists, and conservatives were battling, not over social change, but to what degree it would occur. Among the economic lower classes (which was most of the country) things were always hard but always continuing to improve. Americans were concerned with things far more provincial, entertaining, progressive, and certainly safer than world war.

Scott Joplin's release of "Maple Leaf Rag" in 1899 had brought ragtime music into the mainstream of American popular culture. Ragtime was no longer music limited to the country's black communities and in 1914 it was still as popular as ever. You could even listen to it in the comfort of your home, playing a recording on your own Victrola. The musical transitions moved onto the dance floor as well, with the waltz and the two-step replacing the cotillion as the country's most popular dances.

If music and dance weren't enough, one could always go to the local nickelodeon, plunk down five cents, and watch the "flickers," so named for the poor quality of film with its moving pictures constantly flickering and often causing headaches. Movies and serial shorts, while silent and requiring the frequent changing of reels, were incredibly popular. So much so, that local "movie houses" started popping up on almost every street corner.

Many were nothing more than vacant storefronts that had wooden chairs, benches, or even pews for seating. The lighting (if any) was atrocious; there was rarely any circulating air, and the "projection screen" was usually nothing more than a sheet of cloth or muslin. But despite these shortcomings, they were affordable to the public, valued entertainment, and exceptionally lucrative to their owners. Chicago, led by Essanay Studios, was the filming location and production capital for the world's movies at the time.

Vaudeville and the "legitimate" theatre allowed patrons to see and hear in person everything from the magic of the Great Houdini to opera's great Enrico Caruso, right down to tawdry comedy acts and exotic oriental dancers. Even the fire at Chicago's famed Iroquois Theatre in 1903, which claimed over 600 lives and had long since been relegated to ancient history, didn't discourage people from filling theatres to capacity.

Americans were enjoying every modern convenience. Horses were being replaced by automobiles and streetcars. For Americans fortunate enough to work at Ford Motor Company in 1914, the booming that year began not in August but in January. What's more, it was not with guns but with dollars.

Henry Ford revolutionized the thinking of America's business community when he announced that he would pay his workers the lavish sum of $5.00 per day (roughly doubling his average worker's pay)! And while the workweek was still six days long, the number of work hours on Ford's assembly line was reduced from nine per day to eight. It was done with the belief that a happier worker would be a more productive worker and would use part of his increased wages to buy the high quality product he produced. As a result of Ford's mass production and shared wealth, the sale of his "Tin Lizzies" reached new heights, and automobiles moved from being play things for the wealthy to a near common necessity.

Communication had long since progressed from the telegraph to the telephone, and by 1914 many urban homes in America, and virtually every business, had a telephone. Cross country travels, as well as suburb to city commutes, were now done in the comfort of modern rail cars, and electric lighting displaced nighttime darkness in homes, factories, and along streets.

The nation's political direction and fortunes had changed recently and manifested themselves at the ballot box. The Progressive movement was again in full swing in the United States. During the presidential election of 1912, Democrat Woodrow Wilson was elected to the White House. His most popular opponent in that three-way race was not the incumbent president, Republican William Howard Taft, but former President Theodore Roosevelt who ran as the nominee of the new Progressive Party.

Taft had been Roosevelt's handpicked successor in 1908, but Roosevelt disagreed with Taft's policies and style of governance and challenged his re-election bid in the Republican primaries of 1912. Roosevelt won nearly all of those primary contests, but Taft was able to use federal patronage to secure the convention delegates necessary for his re-nomination. Roosevelt stormed out of the Republican convention, accepted the nomination of the Progressives (Bull Moose Party), and promptly split the Republican vote ensuring Wilson's election.

Roosevelt could take some satisfaction in the fact that he received more votes than Taft (the only time in an American presidential election in which a third party candidate garnered more votes than a major party nominee). Wilson espoused progressive ideals in a pragmatic way but was too shrewd to reveal publicly that he was far more an ideologue than a pragmatist.

Pure Progressive ideology contained a healthy dose of populism and class warfare. It espoused a much bigger role for centralized (federal) government that included higher tax rates, especially for corporations, and using that authority in support of labor unions. They also took a liberal stance on social issues: racial equality, woman's suffrage, and support for Darwin's theory of evolution.

Ironically, though Wilson had been Governor of New Jersey, he was a native of Virginia, lived for a few years in South Carolina, and then in Georgia. He was a racial bigot and chauvinistic toward women. He paid only lip service to the civil rights and suffrage movements of the day, but this served his political purposes well. As Joseph P. Kennedy, father of President John Kennedy once said, "In politics, perception is reality." In sum, Wilson had far more interest in domestic issues than foreign affairs.

Most Americans supported a progressive agenda, in varying degrees, but tempered with a healthy dose of social morality (seemingly odd by modern political standards). This was evidenced by growing support for things like the prohibition of alcohol, along with widespread opposition (even among Protestants) to Margaret Sanger and her advocacy of birth control.

Wilson's Secretary of State was William Jennings Bryan. A pacifist, populist, and class warrior extraordinaire, Bryan had been the unsuccessful presidential nominee of the Democratic Party in 1896 (he was simultaneously the nominee of the Populist Party that year), 1900, and 1908. Now, at a time of war in Europe, he was the nation's most influential man in determining America's foreign policy.

Wilson and his policies received an endorsement of sorts when the Democrats kept their congressional majorities in the mid-term elections of 1914, due in no small measure to the presence of Progressive Party candidates on the ballot who again split the Republican vote.

But even with certain domestic political divisions, much of America in 1914 was relatively peaceful and nearly everyone was in favor of neutrality. In May of that year, Wilson signed a resolution passed by congress declaring the second Sunday in May as "Mother's Day." The country was urged to show support for their mothers by displaying the nation's flag from the front of their homes.

There was some unrest as Jacob Coxey tried, but failed, to form a second "Coxey's Army" (of the poor and unemployed) to march on Washington and demand financial relief for their plight. This had been done before, during the depression of 1894, but the industrial boom that America had been experiencing since before the Civil War had increased wages by roughly 75% over the previous sixty years, and so Coxey's effort fizzled out.

Child labor was still a problem, with children under the age of 10 working in factories and mines and experiencing the horror of industrial accidents, but this was accepted as a norm of the times, with many believing that the need for formal education ended once a child had learned the three R's; "reading, 'riting, and 'rithmatic." *colon !*

Americans, while desiring neutrality for reasons already stated, had also shown throughout their history that they were not afraid to fight Europeans. They had fought two wars with Britain in their national infancy. The first when the thirteen colonies had won their independence (with essential French help) after a protracted eight-year struggle (1775–1783) in which the British decided that their cost for victory could not be justified by the necessary expenditure of blood and treasure.

During the start of the Napoleonic Wars, America fought a quasi, or undeclared naval war, with France for two years (1798–1800). The semi-hostilities between the two countries originated when the United States concluded a trading agreement with Great Britain, France's mortal enemy. Insult was added to injury when the U.S. refused to repay its war debts to Republican France, saying the money was owed instead to the now defunct French monarchy.

The French responded by seizing cargo from American ships on the high seas, and before long it was common practice for French and American ships to fire at one another on sight. A diplomatic solution was reached before the matter escalated into a full-blown war.

America fought its "second war for independence" and became an unintentional ally of Napoleonic France when it declared war against Britain in June of 1812. Britain's great military might rested primarily in its navy and, since it had a manpower shortage and did not recognize the right of its own people to become naturalized American citizens, it began the process of simply impressing any American on the high seas it suspected of being from the commonwealth into the British Navy. This outrage, along with the less noble desire of American war hawks to acquire Canada, led the United States to declare war against Britain.

This second conflict between America and Britain ended without a victor after Russian urgings for negotiation eventually resulted in the Treaty of Ghent. The warring parties signed the peace treaty in December of 1814, but it took considerable time for news to cross the Atlantic.

In the meantime, the war continued unabated in the United States. When the British sent a large force to seize the port city of New Orleans in January of 1815, it was repulsed by American General (and future president) Andrew Jackson in one of the most lopsided military victories in history. In America, the news of the victory at New Orleans was followed immediately by the news of peace, which left almost every American mistakenly believing—even to this day—that the United States had "won" the war.

The United States won a decisive victory against the decaying Spanish Empire during a brief five-month conflict in 1898. The Spanish-American War, often referred to as, "that splendid little war," resulted in the U.S. acquiring the Philippine Islands and Puerto Rico from Spain, while obtaining independence for Cuba. From the most powerful Empire in Europe, and probably the world, to one whose glory was now only a memory, Americans had taken on and defeated Europeans.

Closer to home, President Wilson militarily assisted the efforts to overthrow the government of Mexican President, and dictator, Victoriano Huerta in 1914. This meant America was choosing sides amidst the continuous revolutions, counter-revolutions and civil war occurring in Mexico.

Using the opportunity of an insult to U.S. honor, (nine U.S. sailors were taken into custody at Tampico while collecting fuel supplies but released almost immediately), Wilson ordered American sailors and marines to seize the city of Vera Cruz when the Mexicans did not apologize in the manner prescribed by the U.S. This effectively denied Huerta a prized port city and its many revenues. The city remained occupied for seven months by U.S. forces, until November of 1914, with war between Mexico and the U.S. narrowly averted.

Unfortunately, the American intervention did considerable damage to diplomatic relations between the two countries and would come back to haunt the U.S. in the near future. In September of 1914, two months before the American occupation of Vera Cruz ended, revolutionary leaders Emiliano Zapata of the south, and Pancho Villa of the north, broke with their Revolutionary Premier, Venustiano Carranza, over his refusal to support their radical "social reforms." Zapata and Villa now harbored a growing resentment over American intervention in general and for the de facto support it lent Carranza in particular. The following year U.S. Marines would occupy Haiti to maintain order and protect American financial interests, after the assassination of Haitian President Vilbrun Guillaume Sam.

The current war in Europe brought reports of German atrocities in occupied Belgium, which angered Americans, but the blockade of Germany by the Brits seemed to even out public opinion. Irish-Americans were large in number and most were faithful Catholics, detesters of England, and Democrats. This undoubtedly made easier the desire of Wilson, a Democrat, to keep the United States officially neutral.

When Germany's U-20 shot a torpedo into the side of the British passenger liner *Lusitania* on May 7, 1915, sending 1,198 civilians, including 128 Americans, to the sea bottom off the Irish coast, U.S. opinion began shifting noticeably toward the Allies. But the shift was only an academic matter, insofar as it helped determine who to cheer for from the sidelines. President Wilson, and one Leonard ("Len") Fairfield, certainly were not convinced that American entry into the war was now a necessary thing.

While Len was no German sympathizer (he was of English-Irish ancestry), he couldn't help but smell a rat when it came to the *Lusitania*'s sinking. He wondered if the British hadn't intentionally baited a hook and dangled it right in front of the Germans. With the Germans foolish enough to take that bait, the Americans might well be ready enough to enter the war on the Allied side.

The Germans had placed ads in over 50 newspapers warning those traveling abroad that the ship was in danger of submarine attack. The ship, while civilian, was always rumored to be carrying Allied war materials, and despite the fact that German subs were known to be operating off the Irish coast, the British specifically denied any destroyer escort to the *Lusitania* as it approached the war zone.

Wilson protested the attack but stated that in regards to America, there was such a thing as a nation being, "too proud to fight." Len described things less nobly and felt the issue was more cut and dry. The Germans may have taken the bait but he and the American public had not. For the moment at least, all remained right, or at least stable, in Len's world. Wilson did not take the country to war over the sinking of the *Lusitania* and that was fine with him. His life up to this point had been a very hard one and he certainly didn't think war would make it any easier.

LEN WAS BORN IN Chicago on November 7, 1892 to Frank and Agnes Fairfield. His father Frank was not, and would never become, an American citizen. Born in Lambeth, Surrey (London) in 1859, he came to America in his teens and took up residence in Chicago where he worked as what the census taker listed as a "can maker." He was not a licensed chemist, but earned a few extra coins mixing his own cold creams and salves that he sold himself.

Baptized in the Anglican Church, he accepted a conversion to Catholicism as necessary in order to marry Agnes O'Brien in August of 1884. He received a conditional baptism into the Catholic faith a month before his wedding. The couple had five children; two girls, followed by Len, and then two more boys. The Fairfield clan, which included Catherine O'Brien, Agnes' widowed mother, lived at 913 South 59th Street on Chicago's Southside. While he became a devout Catholic, Frank never gave up singing his beloved Protestant hymns, which he did frequently while sitting and rocking in the privacy of the home's attic. He refused American citizenship because he could never bring himself to renounce the crown.

Unfortunately, Frank had a serious drinking problem, was known to wander from home for periods, and was not an adequate provider. Len had to help support the family and was unable to continue his education beyond elementary school. He refused to attend his graduation ceremony because he had no proper shoes to wear. He spent a fair portion of what should have been his time for youthful folly walking along the railroad tracks picking up coal, often thrown intentionally from trains by kind-hearted rail workers for the poor and destitute, to bring home for heat.

While anti-Catholic feelings ran strong amongst many Protestants of the era, Len remained grateful all his life to the Salvation Army for the charity and assistance they extended to the Fairfield household. They never questioned the faith of those in need. They simply helped.

Len had a handsome face with a Roman nose, gray eyes, and brown hair. He did not have a large frame. As he grew into manhood, he was not quite 5'8" tall and wore a mere size seven shoe, but what he lacked in physical stature he more than made up for with mental ability. He possessed an exceptionally strong natural aptitude for mechanical items, engineering, and mathematics.

Len studied on his own at the local library to prepare himself to pass an examination to become a stationary engineer. He was a rugged individualist in the most traditional sense and saw education as the means to a better life. His study and work drew dividends as he went on to pass a certification exam as a stationary engineer. He then secured a job as a "valveman" at People's Gas and Lite, usually known simply as the "gas works," at 9541 South Baltimore Avenue in Chicago. He worked the midnight to 7:00 a.m. shift. His duties included the reading and recording of valves and gauges, making any necessary adjustments, and at the end of his shift phoning in a full report of his activities to the administrative office.

Despite this newfound promise in steady work, tragedy seemed to be stalking Len. He came home from work on Tuesday morning, June 27, 1911, and realized he had forgotten his key. He knocked on the door and his 77-year-old grandmother, Catherine, started down the second floor stairs to let him in. She never made it. While descending the stairs, she fell and broke her neck. To make matters worse, she survived in agony in her own bed as a quadriplegic for another eight days before succumbing to complications. Len not only lost his beloved grandmother but would carry a strange sense of guilt, perhaps greater than any artillery related death he would inflict on the German enemy, for the rest of his life.

The tragedy probably sparked a need for new surroundings, and the Fairfields moved to a full floor apartment at 1009 W. 55th Street. It was pleasant neighborhood on the Southside with a beautiful midway (park) that separated the east and westbound traffic lanes from each other. The neighborhood was again poor, but like its residents, very clean and proud.

In 1916 there was more trouble between Mexico and the U.S. which increased the potential for war between the two nations. Mexico's revolutionary struggles had been going on since 1910 and Pancho Villa, a revolutionary general (or opportunistic bandit depending on one's point of view) in the north of Mexico, brought his troops across the border into Columbus, New Mexico on March 9th in retaliation for America's support of Carranza, and also to seize guns and ammunition for his army. He was quickly routed by the U.S. 13th Cavalry and suffered 80 dead among his ranks. There were also 17 Americans killed in the incident. There was a large clamor from the American public for an immediate response.

General John J. Pershing, future commander of the American Expeditionary Force (AEF) in Europe, was directed by President Wilson (with enthusiastic permission from Carranza's government) to lead a force into Mexico to take Villa. It was known as the "Punitive Expedition" and it boosted American resolve and morale. It also served as a training maneuver to prepare American officers, like George Patton, and enlisted personnel for future fighting in Europe. The Punitive Expedition did not bring about a definitive battle with Villa, but the United States won a number of smaller skirmishes including one at San Miguelito Ranch, where Lieutenant George Patton led America's first motorized attack using three Dodge touring cars with machine guns mounted in the rear of each auto. Patton killed Julio Cardenas, Villa's second in command, and the Expedition succeeded in keeping Villa away from American soil.

The presidential election of 1916 focused primarily on the war in Europe. Republican Nominee Charles Evans Hughes, with the support of Theodore Roosevelt, who left the Progressives and returned to the Republican fold, was saber rattling and blasting Wilson for being weak.

Wilson largely ignored his domestic agenda and let his campaign slogan, "He kept us out of war," do his talking for him. Len, not an enthusiastic supporter of either candidate, sided with Wilson over peace and breathed a sigh of relief when he was ever-so-narrowly re-elected. Peace was a campaign promise Len wanted and expected to be fulfilled. Things, at least momentarily, seemed to have calmed again but the contentment Len and the nation were sharing would not last long.

On February 1, 1917 the Germans announced that they were resuming their previous policy of unrestricted submarine warfare. This was intended to starve England into submission. The policy directed German U-boats to sink any ships, from neutral as well as belligerent nations, bound for any English port. Americans regarded this as a violation of the free seas and as a hostile act against their right to trade with whomever they pleased. As a result, the United States severed diplomatic relations with Germany on February 3rd.

Still, some invoked America's third President, Thomas Jefferson, who had ordered a self-imposed embargo that he had used, at least initially, to keep the United States out of conflict at the height of the Napoleonic Wars. Jefferson reasoned that if no American ships were on the high seas then there would be no incidents with the British or French navies. It was not a popular act. The American people made a palindrome out of Jefferson's embargo, referring to it as the, "O-Grab-Me." Jefferson later said that he felt the very pillars of government shake under his feet. It did not seem a more viable option 110 years later.

Any hope of negotiating with the German Empire over their submarine warfare policies was lost a month later. On March 1st, the Zimmermann Telegram hit the American public like a bombshell. It was the British who made certain that the intercepted (and coded) telegram made its way into American hands.

German Foreign Secretary Arthur Zimmermann was offering a formal military alliance to Mexico. Together they would make war against the United States (getting Japan to join them if possible) and, once victorious, Mexico would reacquire much of the American southwest—namely, the states of Texas, Arizona and New Mexico lost to the U.S. after the Mexican-American War of 1846–48. Mexico, having had its national eagle thoroughly plucked by the U.S. in war seventy years earlier, never seriously considered the offer, but the national outrage on America's part could not be mollified.

There was no question now that Wilson was going to ask congress for a declaration of war against Germany and that he would get it. Most Americans felt the country's back was against the wall and that war was the only alternative. Wilson, now apparently willing to swallow the pride that had kept him from fighting after the *Lusitania*'s sinking, would lead the country into war because, in his words, "the world must be made safe for democracy."

At the time, Len was dating and becoming serious with an exceptional young woman of German descent. With good looks, intellect, and a fine personality, Gretchen seemed to be everything he could want in a wife save for one thing—she wasn't a Catholic. She was Lutheran, and he worried desperately that marrying her could jeopardize his faith. He was praying hard for direction, and if that meant ending that relationship for another, as good or better with a Catholic, then so be it.

God apparently didn't wait long to answer his prayers. In March of 1917 he went to make his customary call to the gas works' administrative office with his morning report when he mistakenly got connected to the Western Union office at 811 W. Jackson. The operator who took the call was a young Irish spitfire by the name of Margaret ("Maggie") Noonan. Maggie was a woman incredibly well matched for Len. She was highly intelligent and a quick study. A real cutie; she had brown hair and eyes. Her eyes could captivate with a look that Clara Bow would envy. She exuded self-confidence but remained sweet and demure. She was every inch a lady, kind and generous. She was practical but did not hesitate to take a risk when deemed appropriate. Her courage never failed her.

She was born on May 3, 1896 in Ballymoe, Ireland to William and Margaret (Wilkinson) Noonan. At 5'4" she was petite but quite attractive with a slender frame and dark features. Like the Kennedys of Boston, she always insisted that her family was "Black Irish." The Black Irish (a term only used outside of Ireland) were said to be the descendants of the Spanish who made their way to the Irish shores after the Armada went down in a storm in 1588. The Irish provided these fellow Catholics with shelter and eventually intermarried with them. The Irish, always poor but proud, insisted that this produced a breed far superior to the red haired and freckled Irish of Nordic descent.

Maggie was the second of six children and her family moved from Ballymoe to Galway when her father was promoted to serve there as the head constable. He had a convenient habit of leaving the list of names of IRA members to be rounded up in that evening's surprise raids in plain view on the kitchen table. His wife then glanced it over before dashing about spreading a warning to most of the intended quarry. Small wonder few of the fugitives were ever apprehended.

There were few opportunities for a stable middle class existence for Catholic girls living in poverty stricken and English occupied Ireland, so Maggie leapt at the suggestion she go to America. Her mother had a brother, Paul Wilkinson, who had previously immigrated to the U.S. He had a steady job as a streetcar conductor in Chicago and could sponsor her coming to America. He agreed to keep an eye on Maggie and find her a descent place to stay. *sp!*

On October 23, 1913, at the tender age of 17, Maggie left Ireland aboard the *S.S. Dominion* and on November 4th docked in Philadelphia, her family having wanted her to avoid the cattle-like conditions at Ellis Island. She took the train from Philadelphia to Chicago and was met by her Uncle Paul, from whom she got her first streetcar ride (free of charge naturally). He had arranged for her to stay in a rented room in the home of a widowed dressmaker by the name of Keeney. The luck of the Irish followed Maggie to America, as days after her arrival a young woman came to Mrs. Keeney to have a wedding dress made. Maggie was present and struck up a conversation with the young bride to be.

The woman confided to her that marriage would, of course, require her to quit her job at Western Union, and though she had already told her supervisor, no one else knew, as it was to be a carefully guarded secret. Maggie discreetly asked the address of the Western Union office. The next day, a 17-year-old Irish immigrant who had only ridden a streetcar once before, knew nothing about getting around the city of Chicago, and had never in her life even used a telephone, was on her way to Western Union to apply for a job!

A police officer explained to her which streetcar to take and how to follow the address numbers on the buildings. She found 811 W. Jackson without any difficulty. The directory in the foyer listed Western Union on the eighth floor. Her heart raced as she rode the elevator up to her destination. As she exited the elevator, there was an almost deafening clattering of typewriters. Maggie saw maybe 50 women typing telegrams and messages at neatly spaced desks in two long rows. There were other women operating switchboards awash in lights and mixed cables. It was almost overwhelming.

She soon found herself before a woman named Mrs. Moffet, the Superintendent/Chief Operator, who asked Maggie how she could be of service. Maggie stated the reason she had come. Mrs. Moffet was stunned to learn that Maggie knew of the pending opening and though she wasn't prepared to conduct a job interview, she consented to the eager young applicant's desire for one. During the conversation, Maggie had to reveal that she did not know how to type, had never used a telephone, knew nothing of national or local geography, and had only been in the country for a week. When she had exhausted all the logical reasons as to why she shouldn't be given the job, Mrs. Moffet simply said, "Well, at least you speak English." Mrs. Moffet took Maggie's address and phone number and said she would consider the matter. Three weeks later Mrs. Moffet called the Keeney house and offered Maggie a job as an operator. They would train her in what she needed to know.

Her training lasted six months and she worked an eight-hour shift that ran from 3:00 p.m. to 11:00 p.m. It was a slower shift and gave her ample time to learn the ropes, including both switchboard operation as well as typing. A year or so later she was assigned to work from 7:00 a.m. to 3:00 p.m. It was this shift that gave her the opportunity to answer a fateful wrong number. It came on March 18, 1917, after she had been on the job for a little over three years.

"Western Union," Maggie announced as she answered the call. "I thought I was dialing the gas company," said the male voice on the other end. "Sorry, you have a wrong number," she said sweetly. "Please wait," he answered. "I think I have the right number."

The two flirted for a few moments, and then Maggie said it was not permitted for employees to have personal phone conversations on the job. "Please give me your home number," he asked. It was against all the rules, maybe even her better judgment, but she gave him the number for the

Keeney home. Maggie was gutsy but modest and the entire event seemed surreal. Their regular phone conversations tied up the Keeney line but drew the two of them ever closer together.

Mrs. Keeney had previously tried to play matchmaker for Maggie and had arranged for her to visit her nephew Herman who had a farm in Wisconsin. Herman was rugged and blond. Herman was a very handsome man of German stock but Maggie found no chemistry between them and was content to leave rural living back to those in Ireland. She had a taste of big city life and preferred it. She soon left Mrs. Keeney's home and moved in with her Uncle Paul and his new bride Margaret Clancy. The two had married primarily to provide a stable home for Maggie.

Maggie felt it was now time to meet face-to-face with her telephone suitor. Len had just been made a Fourth Degree in the Knights of Columbus and would be attending an installation dinner in the Chicago loop (the elevated train tracks form a loop around the downtown area of Chicago even to this day). Len's sister Mary would also be going. Maggie accepted the invitation with gusto.

Maggie's Uncle Paul and Aunt Margaret thought that she and her new beau had met at Western Union. Maggie played along; after all, what kind of a girl would agree to go out with a man she'd only known through telephone conversations? What's more, he had an English surname (Fairfield). Even if he was Catholic, this was an unpardonable offense to a native of Ireland, even if that native's own surname (Wilkinson) was English!

Maggie did nothing to correct her aunt and uncle's misconception that they had met at Western Union. She said Len's surname was Fitzgerald, and since he was a Fourth Degree (her Uncle Paul was only a Third Degree), her overseers were duly impressed. The evening was a great success and it was as close to love at first sight as one could imagine. They continued to talk on the phone and see each other when their conflicting work schedules allowed. It was a whirlwind romance. It was also the spring of 1917 and love, like war, was clearly in the air.

The two young lovers were jolted back into reality when on April 2nd, world events overtook them and Wilson addressed congress requesting a declaration of war against Germany and her allies. Four days later Congress approved it and America became the "Associated Power."

Wilson, a nanny by nature, narcissistic and naïve beyond words, believed he always knew best and espoused with an air of superiority that America had no territorial claims or interests in entering the war. He insisted on a clear distinction, clarifying that the United States was simply "associated" with those already at war with Germany, rather than actually allied with them. America had its own reasons for going to war, with the first among those reasons being to make the world safe for democracy; its role as world policeman had officially been launched.

In the midst of all this international intrigue Maggie's aunt and uncle decided to celebrate her 21st birthday (May 3rd) in style. There was to be a party at home featuring a roast beef dinner with all the trimmings—a cake with 21 candles and a special invitation to Len, this fine broth of an Irish man she was dating. Len had a dozen roses sent to Maggie that afternoon and gave her their first kiss that evening. Fate would not allow this bliss to go unchallenged; America had just recently gone to war and both of these young lovers would soon feel its effects.

The United States may have declared war, but it was woefully unprepared to wage it. Since the American Army had not quite 130,000 men in its ranks in early 1917, the Selective Service Act (conscription) was passed on May 18th. If Len and Maggie had had any illusions that they may have been overlooked by these catastrophic events as two mere specks of insignificant humanity, those illusions were certainly shattered now.

The new conscription law called for registration and drafting to occur in stages. It mandated the registration of all males living in the U.S. regardless of citizenship status. The first registration was conducted on "National Draft Day" which was Tuesday, June 5, 1917 and was for men born between June of 1886 and June of 1896 (those aged 21 to 31 at the time). By the third and final registration in September of 1918, a total of 24 million men had completed the process, with the age for registrants having gone all the way up to age 46!

Len, American by birth, in excellent heath and born in 1892, was among almost 10 million men who registered for the draft on June 5th. Those who did not register on National Draft Day soon received the infamous "red postcard" ordering them to register lest they be in violation of federal law and subject to arrest and prosecution.

Len had to report to the draft board at 5507 South Halsted Street, one of 86 such boards in Chicago and 4,000 in the nation, the following month for an interview. He was single, healthy, and 24 years old, so naturally the draft board deemed him to be immediately eligible for military service. He was directed to report for a physical examination that he passed with ease.

In mid-August, the notorious "blue postcard" arrived in Len's mail informing him that he had to be ready to report for military service within 24 hours of receiving any official notice sent to him. That notice came a few days later and he and Maggie said their goodbyes. He headed off for the armory at 2643 W. Madison Avenue on Chicago's Westside prepared to enter military service.

The armory was impressive beyond words. Built in 1916, it was home to the 132nd Infantry Regiment of Illinois' 33rd Infantry Division (National Guard). It was a behemoth structure. It's composition, brick and steel, inspired a sense of security and permanence. It spanned a full city block in length, running from Madison Avenue south all the way over to Monroe. Both streets had grand entrances.

The gymnasium, pools, and most of its other amenities were open to the public, but its drill facilities were state of the art and truly amazing. They were in the center of the building in a hall five stories high supported by steel trusses and complete with a skylight that ran the entire length of the ceiling allowing for natural light during the day. The building included indoor rifle and pistol ranges as well as showers, lockers and seemingly anything else that came to mind. It often hosted recreational events for civilians and was a sight that could not help but awe.

Some of Maggie's Irish luck must have rubbed off on Len because when he arrived for induction he and those reporting with him learned, to their utter amazement and joy, that due to the large number of recruits (volunteers and draftees) the army could not yet process them all; he was among those who had a brief reprieve until the next round of inductees would be called up. He and Maggie continued to date over the following weeks and to fall more deeply in love.

Len received a second notice at the end of September that he would be officially inducted and processed at the armory on October 1st. He reported as instructed, completed the necessary paperwork, and was grouped together with other recruits as he raised his right hand and took the oath, officially making him a soldier in the United States Army. The men were then informed that they would be released for the remainder of the day, and for the following day as well, to say final goodbyes and settle any outstanding civilian business. They had to report back to the armory by 7:00 a.m. on October 3rd or face arrest for desertion.

This momentary parole from the army provided Len with a chance to do what he previously only dreamt of doing—marrying Maggie! The couple had spent much of his August/September reprieve talking about marrying before he entered the service. Now, this brief window of opportunity would be the time they needed to do just that.

Len contacted Maggie as soon as he left the armory and proposed marriage. They decided immediately to see Maggie's parish priest, Father Tom O'Hara, at Corpus Christi Church to see if it could be done. Father O'Hara was sympathetic to the young couple and since they were both of age (Len was 24 and Maggie 21), the priest agreed to marry them the following day if they had their marriage license.

Maggie's aunt and uncle would never approve of a whirlwind romance ending in a marriage that was a virtual elopement. She knew this all too well, so the couple decided to keep their wedding a closely guarded secret. The following day they went to the Cook County Clerk's office and obtained a wedding license. It was valid for 30 days but the young lovers had no intention of waiting beyond that afternoon to wed.

A close personal friend of Len's served as his best man. Maggie had a friend, Mae from Western Union, serve as her maid of honor. Father O'Hara performed a simple ceremony at Corpus Christi Church with no mass. It was all over in about 20 minutes.

The newlyweds and their "bridal party" of two took the elevated train downtown for lunch and a variety show at the Hippodrome Theatre. After the show, everyone parted company as Maggie went to spend the night with Mae while Len and his best men each headed for their respective homes.

They were married now, though their families knew nothing about it. The couple had no way of knowing when, or even if, they would ever see each other again. For the two of them, the effects of war had come to

America and swept over them like an ocean wave. In less than a year, Len would be pulled out with it as it returned bound for Europe and the "war to end all wars."

Doughboys being trained in the use of gas masks. Most American soldiers and Marines used the British Small Box Respirator (SBR) like those pictured. The mask had a snorkel-like piece that was inserted into the mouth and a clip that went over the nose. Doughboys had to have short haircuts and close shaves for a proper fit, and were trained to have the mask on in six seconds or less.

CHAPTER 2

. . . .

Arriving, Training, and Departing Camps Grant and Logan

AFTER A QUICK ROLL call to verify attendance, Len and the other new recruits departed the armory and "marched," suitcases in hand, roughly three miles east down Madison Avenue before turning south onto Canal Street. Their destination was the Union Depot (Union Station after being rebuilt in 1925) where they boarded the Chicago Burlington and Quincy Railroad, known simply as the Burlington, or just the "Q".

The train took them from downtown Chicago to Rockford and arrived just outside the immediate boundaries of Camp Grant around noon on October 3, 1917. Upon arrival, Len and the others were quickly sectionalized and given their first assignments to a unit.

Like many of the men arriving at Camp Grant, Len was initially assigned to the 86th Infantry ("Blackhawk") Division. He was a part of Company H of the 341st Regiment. He wouldn't stay in the 86th very long, as few did. The 86th Division was never deployed in World War I; served as an organization for induction with 186,000 men passing through its ranks on their way to other units. To say that Camp Grant had been hastily, but skillfully, put together would have been an understatement. It was a military miracle of rapid planning, logistics, engineering, and execution. It was a tragedy that this miraculous degree of government efficiency didn't translate into weapons production and combat readiness.

The United States had entered the war in April of 1917, and just two months later one of the country's largest facilities for induction, processing, and basic training started to spring into life. The U.S. Government decided that the area immediately south of Rockford, Illinois would be an ideal locale, due to its central position in the Midwest and its role as both a rail and river hub. More than 8,000 workers swooped down on the area to construct roughly 1,100 buildings in less than six months! The camp would have the ability to house roughly 50,000 military personnel in an area of just over 5,600 acres.

Uncle Sam was going all out for his boys, having paid almost a million dollars for the property and another seven million for the camp's construction and operation. Along with the traditional hospital, dental facilities, barracks, mess halls, officers' club, post office, and Red Cross buildings, there was a library, theaters, and YMCA buildings. The YMCA made stationary and envelopes available to the soldiers free of charge. Soldiers were strongly encouraged to write home often and Len did. He wrote Maggie almost every day.

There were theater buildings for the Knights of Columbus, the YMCA, and even the "Liberty Theater" which could seat 4,500! These theatres presented the vaudeville shows of the day, and included magic acts, dance acts, jazz music, singers (usually patriotic in the tradition of George M. Cohan), comedy routines and even black-faced minstrels. Other performers, such as acrobats and pugilists (boxers), were normally outdoor features. Camp Grant included steam heat, an ice plant, power plant, a remount depot capable of accommodating 5,000 horses and mules, a school for blacksmiths, and even its own fire department. In short, it was as modern and convenient as most any fair-sized town at the time, and probably provided better living accommodations than a number of its occupants had ever experienced before.

There was next to nothing in the way of public transportation from Camp Grant into Rockford, so entrepreneurial civilians filled the void using their personal automobiles as taxis. A one-way trip from either location to the other cost 25 cents for civilians and 15 cents for those in military uniform.

The barracks were wooden frame, immensely large, two story buildings. Each barrack held 200 men. The men slept in single bunks on the second floor. The first floor served as the mess hall and recreation room. A kitchen was present on the first floor, but if necessary, mobile "rolling kitchens"—essentially an oven mounted on an open wagon—would be set up just outside when larger quantities of hot food were prepared.

A month before Len's arrival, former President Theodore Roosevelt, the Rough Rider and hero of the Spanish-American War, (Roosevelt would be posthumously awarded the nation's highest military decoration, the Medal of Honor, in 2001) gave an inspiring address to the troops at the camp. It was probably just as well that Len missed it. He was not only a conscript, but somewhat less than certain that America should even be involved in the war. He was also 24 years old and newly married. He didn't share the starry-eyed idealism, dreams of glory, or a hunger for combat possessed by many of the younger recruits and war hawks. Still, he was there, and as always, could be counted on to carry out whatever responsibilities life sent his way.

The new recruits were sent to the Supply Service (Quartermaster) where they were issued the first part of their uniforms. America was so totally ill prepared for war that uniforms had to be issued piecemeal with components being distributed as they became available. Len and the other new arrivals received a khaki shirt with two breast pockets and a campaign ("Montana") hat that resembled the state police hats of modern day.

This was certainly not a haberdashery (although the troops were charged for their uniforms) nor the ideal of military proficiency, as each recruit was simply handed whatever shirt and hat the issuer found convenient within his reach on the shelf. The soldiers had to scramble amongst themselves and rapidly swap with one another in a mad dash so they could possess a proper fitting "uniform" before the clock ran out on their half-hour deadline to assemble. After completing the necessary exchanges of shirts and hats, Len and the others assembled on the parade grounds for their initial inspection and orientation. The half-baked uniform (the men were still wearing civilian trousers and shoes), and its wearer, was dubbed, "the casual."

At assembly, the men were ordered to form up, and Len was frustrated by the constant correction to posture, head angle, and even breathing. They were reminded that they were soft civilians and that the army was their new home where they would be made into soldiers. They were for the time being spared military haircuts. That would come soon enough.

Len took the "Army Alpha" IQ test and scored well (the "Beta Test" used pictures and was issued to those illiterate). Because he was a stationary engineer, Len was also administered a "Trade Test" which revealed his strong mathematical skills and mechanical aptitude. With the talents that Len possessed now documented and confirmed, the army decided that he be assigned a specialty other than that of rifleman in an infantry unit. He was an exception. The U.S. Army and the Marine Corps would together raise more than four million men, two million of whom would actually get to France, the vast majority of these being riflemen.

The army now issued the men more of their uniforms; khaki trousers to match the shirt, along with a skin itching wool ensemble of trousers, shirt, pull-over sweater, and coat, all in olive drab. Also issued were brown ankle-high boots and leggings.

During October of 1917, some 5,600 draftees were transferred into the 33rd Infantry ("Prairie") Division that was, and remains today, an Illinois National Guard Unit. It had been federalized for the war on July 18, 1917 and could thus take conscripts. On October 23rd, Len was assigned to one of the Division's artillery units, Battery A of the 124th Field Artillery (FA) Regiment where he would be trained as an artillery scout (today classified as a forward observer or perhaps better known to civilians as an "artillery spotter"). Forward Observer (FO) was not yet classified as a Military Occupational Specialty (MOS) during World War I, but the basic principles of its duties still remain the same in the modern military.

The Manual for Noncommissioned Officers and Privates of Field Artillery of the Army of the United States (1917) states that artillery scouts should be; "alert, cool-headed, intelligent men" and "good horsemen, with good eyesight and good hearing." With the overwhelming majority of recruits being trained as riflemen ("cannon fodder"), it was a real testament to Len's ability that he was selected for this duty.

Many of the men making up the 124th Field Artillery were from Southern Illinois' Sangamon County (Springfield) and East St. Louis. Oddly enough, while the 33rd Division was an Illinois unit, the army in all its infinite wisdom decided (probably for climatic reasons which would turn out to be a great irony) that their training would not take place at Camp Grant in Rockford, Illinois but rather at Camp Logan outside Houston, Texas. Within weeks after their arrival at Camp Grant, they departed by Pullman cars for Camp Logan for their basic and advanced (individual) training.

Soon after their arrival, Len and the other recruits had to say good morning to "Mr. Zip-Zip-Zip." A mechanical haircutting device, it was held in one hand and powered by the operator's physical ability, and resembled more a small pair of pruning sheers rather than a barber's tool. In fact, the assignment to cut hair was given out randomly and few men had their hair cut by actual barbers. The results were painstakingly clear in the men's appearance, as "steps" and uneven cuts were the order of the day. Most men preferred to have their haircut as short as possible for obvious reasons.

Camp Logan's size was similar to that of Camp Grant's, but while most of the military camps in the North had framed buildings, those in the South were merely tent cities. The living quarters of the soldiers, however, were not row upon row of pup tents but fairly sizable canvas shelters that held some eight to ten men each. A few tar-papered shacks also dotted the landscape.

It was here, sharing a tent, that Len became acquainted with Alexander ("Al") Slowey from Chicago. Slowey, like Len, had been drafted. Also like Len, Slowey was a Chicago south sider, from 63rd Street. Before entering the army Slowey had been a clerk for the Chicago & Alton (C&A) Railroad, known for transporting coal, cattle, and passengers almost exclusively between Illinois and Missouri. Al was four years Len's junior but the two were both graduates of the school of hard knocks and shared many common interests and experiences. Almost immediately, they became good friends. Their friendship would last throughout their lives.

Tent living was especially difficult for the Doughboys because the winter of 1917–1918 was ferociously harsh across the entire U.S. The Ohio valley had some of the coldest temperatures in its recorded history and the same was true for much of New England. Houston, where January temperatures usually average between 40 to 60 degrees Fahrenheit, was having its coldest winter in over three decades with temperatures averaging in the teens accompanied by heavy snow!

True to their reputation for ingenuity, Americans adapted to their circumstances. The Doughboys in southern camps would have to heat their tents. They did this by first placing wooden boards over their dirt floors and then boarding the walls inside the tents to a height of some three to four feet. The men were issued a cone shaped piece of heavy stove-type material about two feet high and about eighteen inches wide which was placed in the center of the tent. The "chimney" consisted of piping about four inches thick which rose up to a tapered collar connected to a hole cut in the canvas at the top of the tent. The pipe had a damper with a small hole cut in the bottom of the cone (for airflow) that could be covered when it was not in use. A door was cut into the side to throw in fuel, either wood or coal, whichever was available.

As if the freakishly cold temperatures weren't bad enough, there was a nationwide scarcity of coal. This meant more than no hot water for bathing, as much of the camp's water supply simply froze. Fuel for fires consisted primarily of wood pilfered from the kitchen's supply, or another tent. The kitchens burned up to five cords a night simply to keep the morning oatmeal lukewarm.

Since there were no bricks available to place the stove on, the Doughboys cut an opening in the floor boarding to leave an area of dirt exposed. They then mounted their stoves over the dirt spot on small frames cut from two-by-fours. While the heat that was generated unquestionably saved men from freezing, the potential fire hazards were phenomenal. The wooden framing supporting the stove, or the wooden floors themselves, could easily catch fire, and sparks were quick to ignite the canvas of the tents. The sight of men running from a blazing tent, or scurrying to throw snow, water, or a bucket of sand on their burning floor, was a common one.

During the nights of that horrific winter of 1917–18, in every tent, there was a rotating duty requiring that each man take a one-hour shift watching over the fire so that it never burned unobserved. This allowed everyone else to sleep with the peace of mind that the fire would not die out or start the tent ablaze. They trusted whoever had the watch that he would protect them from a frozen or fiery death. This type of duty (performed in previous wars) is the origin of the military term, "fire watch" where, to the current day, military personnel take their turn completing a one-hour shift of watching over the inside of the barracks while their comrades sleep.

Len's engineering aptitude had given him the foresight to take up a collection and pay one of the blacksmiths to hammer flat some metal piping. He and Al then placed it between the wooden framing along the bottom of their stove to reduce the chance of the frame's igniting. This was the first of a lifetime of Rube Goldberg-like projects that the two men would partner in.

The bitter winter may also have contributed to the increased incidences of flu. The Great Flu Pandemic, also known as the "Spanish Influenza," started in the fall of 1917 and lingered into the spring of 1919. The first year's strain was nowhere near as deadly as the variation that hit the following year. Still, it was starting to wreak havoc around the globe and Camp Logan was no exception. Toward the end of September 1917, over 600 cases of flu had been reported at the camp with a death rate of almost ten percent! Rather than quarantining the ill soldiers, the decision was made to send them home or to civilian hospitals. That only served to spread the infection further into the civilian community and undoubtedly raised the mortality level for those poor souls who were forced to travel while being so ill. These practices continued into 1918.

In an effort to try and control other potentially lethal illnesses, the new recruits were to be administered mandatory protection against diseases such as smallpox, typhoid and paratyphoid. This meant a lengthy and painful series of inoculations. Len and the others resented the total lack of empathy on the part of the physicians who administered these vaccines. The large gauge needles in the hypodermics were pushed roughly into their arms, almost tearing as opposed to puncturing the skin. There was no "darting" of needles or pinching off of skin, and the large quantities of serum rapidly injected into the upper arm displaced muscle and created additional misery to an already painful process. Len had to endure this tortuous procedure once a week for three weeks until the series of injections was complete.

As bad as the typhoid and paratyphoid shots were, the smallpox inoculation was worse as it was delivered in an even less humane way. Glass vials of the vaccine were broken open and the jagged glass from the vials was used to scratch (more often cut) a swath across a soldier's arm. Len

mustered every ounce of courage and self-discipline he possessed. If a soldier fainted, grunted in pain, or even flinched, it always resulted in depre-
cating remarks from the physicians and supervising sergeants along with
some form of retributive treatment. Len wondered if the mid-evil practice
of "bleeding" might be applied for good measure. He and most of the other
recruits felt sick as dogs for weeks after their inoculations. *Medieval?*

If weather and infection hazards weren't bad enough, Camp Logan,
and the City of Houston, were experiencing racial strife far more intense
than usual. The American Army was still racially segregated during both
world wars. On August 23, 1917 there had been a race riot and military
mutiny over controversy surrounding the arrest of a black military policeman by white civilian police in downtown Houston.

One hundred fifty-six black Doughboys from the 24th Infantry Regiment broke into the arms cache at Camp Logan and then marched on the
city, armed and determined to release a man who was in actuality no longer
in custody. The situation was explosive and resulted in significant blood-
letting. When the shooting stopped there were 12 dead civilians, 4 dead
white police, and 4 dead black soldiers. This would later result in 19 black
soldiers being hanged and 63 more given life sentences, all for mutiny in
wartime. This did nothing but aggravate the already serious rift in race
relations, which was national at the time, and kept a strictly enforced cur-
few in effect in Houston. Amazingly, Len managed to avoid freezing, fire,
racial unrest, and the flu while stationed at Camp Logan.

The new recruits at Camp Logan spent eight hours a day in training.
This was done for six days every week with only Sundays and holidays for
rest. Other work assignments, like chopping wood, raking, and cleaning
latrines had to be performed daily but were not considered to be part of
the day's training. Dinner was served at 5:00 p.m. sharp, followed by a few
hours of personal time for reading and letter writing. The playing of Taps
took place at 9:00 pm, followed immediately by lights out.

The next day started with buglers blowing reveille at 5:00 am. That
horrible sound, followed immediately by the sergeants' constant yelling of
"Fall Out! Fall Out!" meant that Len and the others had to instantly leap
from their cots, dress, and assemble in platoons for a morning count to
ensure that everyone was present and accounted for.

The men then marched to their barracks hall, or in southern camps, large field tents where they were fed breakfast, which might include fried potatoes, fresh baked bread, oatmeal, cold cereal, occasionally pancakes, and mud black coffee with condensed milk, and all served in abundance. The men ate out of their mess kits and used their own cup and utensils, swishing them clean after meals in barrels filled with disinfectant. They then had 30 minutes for personal hygiene and that included bathroom, teeth brushing, and shaving time—all necessities whether by order of nature or military regulation.

The overcrowded facilities, limited time, and limited access to water (the latter coming from the small number of hand pumps—when they weren't frozen—spewed into tin bins frequently used simultaneously by several shaving Doughboys), required many a poor soldier to perform an ever so painful "dry shave." Sometimes Len shaved the night before to avoid this hassle. By 6:00 a.m. the soldiers were dressed, fed, clean shaven, and ready to start the day.

The training day began with an hour of calisthenics. These included jumping jacks, sit-ups, push-ups, windmills, squats, leap frog, and other tortuous forms of exercise designed to increase endurance and muscle mass. Calisthenics were not limited to the morning. Then, as now, all military recruits had to learn how to march, use a rifle, and learn some basic infantry tactics, as circumstance can put anyone near the front lines in the center of a fight in the blink of an eye.

American military planners had no real knowledge of the evolution of tactics that had taken place among European armies during the previous three years. Seldom now did Europeans send human waves charging across no man's land through a hail of machine gun fire and artillery shells to attack their opponent. That practice had been almost entirely abandoned by the end of 1917.

Unfortunately, American military planners knew little or nothing of this updating of tactics, and America's strategic and logistical thinkers were seemingly more convinced than ever that all that was needed to break the stalemate on the Western Front was to send men of grit "over the top" to charge across no man's land and destroy the enemy with bayonets fixed on the end of their rifles. It was now 1918 but America was training to go into battle using 1914 tactics. It was something that would needlessly cost thousands of American Doughboys their lives.

To help raw recruits become men of grit, and due to an initial shortage of rifles, most of the American training was endurance related and consisted of repeated regimens of calisthenics followed by long forced marches through dense woods and hilly terrain often with heavy haversacks. It was a matter of personal pride to every recruit not to drop out of these marches no matter how tired they felt or how sore and bloody their feet became.

Len noticed that every time his feet seem to callous up enough to tolerate the marches; the marching distance was extended just enough to ensure that his feet were blood soaked and well blistered at its conclusion. A march of fifteen miles complete with full packs became a ritual performed every Friday (appropriate enough for Catholics who regarded Fridays as a day of abstinence, allowing them to share in the sufferings of the Passion). There was also the constant drill of putting on gas masks as rapidly as possible. This tedious task was practiced with so much repetition that every soldier soon became an expert at having their mask on within six seconds of the warning sound of the klaxon, or after being ordered to put them on by their superiors.

Periods of relief came in the form of ceremonial and close order drill; normally mastered in mere minutes, these drills were tediously performed for hours on end. There was also the constant "policing" (cleaning) of the camp's grounds. All of this undoubtedly being made more miserable by the wearing of itchy wool uniforms.

Mess (indoor) chow was always welcome compared to field rations that were not always reliably issued or delivered, especially for lunch, even at military sites in the United States. Fresh baked bread was prized most. It was cooked in outdoor ovens, the dough poured into molds that formed six loaves all connected at the bottom and then cut into individual loaves after delivery to the mess area. There were hearty servings of baked beans ("bullets") usually with pork chunks and onions. Corned beef hash ("willy") and potatoes were regular staples, often accompanied by stewed tomatoes.

Also served in the mess at dinner was creamed chipped beef on toast, better known as "SOS." The acronym had several meanings: something on a shingle, same old stuff, save our stomachs, and perhaps the best known—"shit on a shingle."

Occasionally on the training grounds Doughboys got a real treat when rolling kitchens, which the soldiers referred to as "soup cannons," would arrive. The troops would race to line up at the barked order to "chow down!" But more often than not the men ate canned foods like willy, sardines, pork, bacon, beans, salmon ("goldfish") and the eternal hard bread—"crackers" that were actually rock hard biscuits that had to be chiseled with a knife, or sucked on, or soaked for long periods before they could be consumed in even the smallest morsels. Len and the others reasoned that hard bread was deliberately intended to cause intense stomach pain so that soldiers couldn't notice how hungry they truly were.

The main difference between the meals served in the mess or from rolling kitchens, compared to the canned rations, was heat. Sternos were seldom available, so artillerymen would demonstrate their ingenuity by using their highly flammable guncotton (if they had it) to make small fires to heat their canned meals. According to legend, Campbell Soups created condensed vegetable soup for soldiers in the field as their contribution to the war effort.

While the United States would eventually send two million men to France, heavy weapons, like artillery pieces, machine guns, planes, and tanks, had to be supplied almost entirely by the British and French.

The standard issue rifle for the U.S. military personnel then was not, as most people think today, the bolt action .30-06 Springfield Model 1903, but in fact was the M1917 Enfield, which is usually referred to as the "American Enfield." Prior to its entry into the war, the "neutral" United States had manufacturers producing Enfield rifles for the British. Rather than attempt to retool factories once war was declared, the government ordered production of a slightly modified version of the British Enfield to enable its use with America's standard .30 caliber round, as well as to avoid patent infringement of the Brits' gun design.

Few American soldiers or marines had the prized Springfield rifles with them when they went into action. There were only 600,000 available when America declared war. Even worse, government arsenals still had countless thousands of the obsolete Krag-Jørgensen rifles left over from the Spanish-

American War twenty years earlier. The Krag-Jørgensen could only hold a single round and had to be reloaded through the breach each time it was fired.

While the rifles of the First World War were all single shot, at least they were bolt-action pieces that were loaded through "stripper clips" that held five rounds of ammunition. A soldier only had to cock the bolt after each shot and could do this five times before having to reload. Obviously, this was a far easier task than the cumbersome process of opening the breach to reload after firing a round.

While Len and the other artillerymen were required to learn how to drill with and use a rifle, they were not, oddly enough, required to qualify on one; thus they had no target scores kept on the practice range and no qualification status issued to them. Since they were trained to ride horses, the artillery scouts carried side arms with them in France, usually the model M1911 Colt .45 caliber semi-automatic pistol. Riding with a rifle slung over one's back is a most difficult feat and relatively pointless for artillery scouts, who were not expected to be in a position where they would be engaging the enemy with rifle fire. *not true today – why would here they?*

The M1911 had demonstrated its exceptional stopping power during the Moro Insurrection in the Philippine Islands. It was a matter of necessity at the time to develop a sidearm that could, with a single hit, bring down a physically large opponent fighting with fanatical determination. The Colt fit the bill nicely.

Despite not being riflemen, Len and the other artillerymen had to participate in thirty minutes a day of bayonet practice. Recruits were reminded that bayonets often remained stuck in their enemy, and soldiers were never to make themselves vulnerable by propping their foot up against an opponent to pull it out. If the bayonet got stuck in the enemy, the soldier removed it in the most practical way—he shot it out!

American frontline soldiers at the time were also issued the M1917 Trench Knife ("Knuckle Duster") which had a triangular shaped stiletto blade able to inflict deep wounds that, when not fatal, were prone to infection and difficult to heal. The big disadvantage of the long thin blade was that it had a tendency to snap off once thrust into an enemy. The knife's handle, or grip, had a thin metal shield covering the user's knuckles.

Something more practical, and effective, was needed.

The M1918 Trench knife had a more traditional blade and the handle had a series of metallic loops that the operator slipped their fingers through ("brass knuckles"), studded with jagged brass edges for maximum damage to the enemy in close quarter combat. Both versions of this gruesome weapon gave Len the shivers and the thought of ever having to use such a thing on another human being was especially unnerving.

Illinois was one of only three states at the time (New York and Pennsylvania being the other two) to have its very own National Guard Division. Illinois Governor and Presidential hopeful, Frank O. Lowden, was not about to miss seeing the men of his "Prairie Division" in training. He travelled to Camp Logan, arriving on November 6th, and immediately began visiting his troops. The following day he and Texas Governor W.P. Hobby reviewed the troops in a ceremonial parade, and as the troops marched past, the two governors were perched comfortably on the balcony of the Rice Hotel in downtown Houston. Lowden spent the next day making more personal rounds with the men of the division before heading back to Illinois. Len was patriotic and no cynic but was never one who was celebrity struck by politicians. He felt their most frequent "accomplishments" were taxes and wars.

After completing their basic training in the middle of January 1918, Len and the others were granted a 10-day leave to return home for a visit. The trip to Chicago was especially unpleasant. The railroad cars were state of the art steel, and the bitter cold of the brutal winter of 1918 made travel in them seem like riding in an icebox on rails.

Len stayed with his new bride who was living in a room at the home of her friend and Western Union co-worker, Mae. Maggie's aunt and uncle had disapproved of her secret ceremony and choice of groom, especially when they found out he had an English surname, so she moved out shortly after her wedding. Since Maggie and Len had had to separate company immediately after their October 2nd wedding, Len's military leave constituted their honeymoon.

There was also time spent with Len's parents and siblings back home on 55th Street. They were now informed that Maggie was no longer Len's sweetheart, but his wife! There were some shocked and bruised egos over the couple's secret wedding, but fortunately for Maggie, she had been held in high regard by the Fairfields since the couple had begun dating. Her natural charm not only enabled her to easily smooth over any miffed feelings, but to quickly win for herself a place of honor in the family. It was plain to see that Len had a good head on his shoulders.

Train travel between Houston and Chicago was time consuming. The days at home passed far too quickly, and all too soon Len was headed back to Camp Logan. Upon his return, Len would begin a program of specialized training as a scout for the field artillery. Prior to the First World War, most artillery pieces were "field guns," capable of firing only in a rifle-like manner. They were aimed and fired directly at clearly visible targets such as advancing enemy troops or a fortress wall. They were normally organized into groups of four guns, each forming what's known as a battery.

World War One saw a massive production and the widespread use of enormous howitzers that were relatively mobile (drawn by horses) and could effectively move with advancing armies. Howitzers have barrels that can be greatly elevated, allowing artillery shells to be shot at very steep angles high into the air at enemy targets, rather than simply being pointed and fired directly. Armies now had the means to fire back and forth at one another's strategic targets, often only a few hundred yards from each other, without the gun crews ever seeing just who or what they were shooting at.

Enter the newly created military specialty of Artillery Scout. It was, and remains today, that individual's job to move to a position well in front of their own lines, or to a great height, where they can effectively spot strategic enemy targets: machine gun nests, pill boxes, dugouts, heavy troop concentrations, and even enemy artillery. He then relays the exact co-ordinates on a map to a friendly artillery battery that promptly begins to bombard the enemy target. The scout also communicates any necessary corrections in the azimuth (a compass heading used to determine an angle of fire), or deflection (leading the target) in the event the target is moving, such as advancing infantry. This allows the scout to skillfully "walk" the barrage squarely onto the target to ensure it's effectively blown to kingdom come.

American artillery scouts received very extensive training in the U.S. that was greatly expanded upon by the French once they arrived in that country. The problem was that their newly acquired knowledge was rendered nearly useless by the technological advances and the circumstances on the battlefields of the Great War.

First was the problem of scouts communicating with their own artillery batteries. Signal flags, gas arc lamps, flare guns, messenger dogs, and carrier pigeons were state of the art military communications at the time, but hardly effective for the rapid communications required in artillery spotting. The first methods mentioned would get the user killed almost the second his communications started, as enemy snipers and artillery could easily spot his location and quickly take him out. Animals, like troops, often became casualties, and that method of relaying messages was simply too slow for artillery use.

The U.S. Army Signal Corps had the 1914 Service Buzzer (field phone) that allowed the operator to communicate by either voice or Morse code, but its signals travelled only by wire. This was problematic since there was a practical limit to the wire's length, and the constant shelling occurring on the battlefields often cut these wires to shreds.

Second were the circumstances on the battlefields. The First World War was largely static in nature, as both sides had trench works that ran parallel to each other, traversing all the way from the English Channel to the Swiss border. Often, the trenches of the warring armies were no more than a few hundred yards apart and the lack of any meaningful cover in the area between them ("no man's land") made it impossible to place observers far out ahead of their own lines.

As far as using high elevations "safely" behind a scout's own lines, bell towers and steeples were routinely shelled into rubble by the opposing side as a precautionary measure, while hills behind the lines were usually pre-sighted by the enemy's artillery and quickly bombarded the moment they were even suspected of being used by a scout.

Finally, there was the fact that while the U.S. did use 155mm French howitzers, the most common artillery gun used by Americans was the French 75mm. It was a very effective piece for direct fire but its barrel had little elevation and the gun literally had to be propped up to provide any substantive change in its angle of fire. This was hardly scientific and certainly not practical.

These conditions often resulted, at least until the final few months of the war, in scouts being placed near their own batteries during battle. While the battery commanders kept their eyes fixed on their assigned objectives, usually infantry, the scouts were busy looking for the muzzle flashes from the enemy's artillery pieces. After spotting them, they would determine their precise location as rapidly as possible and hopefully enable their own gunners to neutralize (destroy) them. This was known as "counter-battery" fire.

Of course, the enemy had their own scouts doing the exact same thing. This circumstance resulted in "artillery duels," in which the batteries of both sides largely ignored the other's infantry and instead blasted away at each other. The side whose scouts were quickest in locating and relaying such information to the battery commander, so that rapid and accurate fire could be brought down upon their foe's guns, obviously "won" the duel. Once the enemy's batteries were obliterated, their infantry became easy prey to artillery fire. Artillery duels are a feature of war that still exists today.

It is interesting to note that most soldiers killed in action during the war did not die by machine gun fire, poison gas, or bayonets, but as a result of artillery fire. Seven out of ten soldiers killed in World War One died as the result of artillery. In fact, artillery inflicted the greatest number of casualties in every major war of the twentieth century. It is no wonder that Napoleon Bonaparte once said, "With artillery, war is made." His comment on the subject would be most prophetic when it came to World War I.

At the time, the initial limitations on artillery scouts were unknown not only to Len, but more importantly to the American tacticians and strategists who naively planned for using highly mobile artillery to assist the infantry during their rapid advances across the battlefields of France.

It was a sad reality that the field artillery of The United States Army was no more prepared for war than any other part of the service. While some of its infantry trained with wooden rifles due to shortages of the genuine item, the field artillery was forced to use a mock version of virtually all its equipment. In fact, the shortage of weapons and horses was so acute that Len's unit was initially trained using "artillery pieces" composed of wooden sticks drawn by "horse teams" that were in actuality men hitched together with twine!

Early in 1918, the 124th finally received a few very fine artillery pieces in the form of 3-inch guns (Model 1902), but Camp Logan did not have an artillery range of its own so the army had to lease a small stretch of property some 10 miles away. It was woefully inadequate as it was long, flat, and narrow. It was more like a bowling lane than an artillery range, but it did familiarize the men with authentic cannon fire. The problem was that the acute shortage of American shipping didn't allow for these guns to be transported to France, so American artillerymen had to be re-trained on French artillery pieces once they arrived in country.

Len began to study vigorously in the classroom and field. Artillery in warfare must be able to do four things in order to properly support its own infantry: effectively determine a target's range, provide accurate fire, maintain a rapid rate of fire, and be highly mobile. In order to be able to perform his duties as a scout, Len would have to learn many things: how to read a military map and use observation tools (binoculars and telescopes) along with land navigation and plotting tools (compass, alidade. etc) so he could identify the position of enemy targets. He needed to be capable of navigating over the moonscapes of no man's lands that were devoid of anything standing. Such circumstances create a condition where one's natural sense of direction is rendered utterly useless.

Len also needed to learn Morse code and how to operate a service buzzer so he could communicate when possible using a field phone. Finally, he had to learn how to care for and ride a horse so he could become quickly mobile when required. All of this training would become considerably more in depth and expanded upon once he got to their school in Ornans, France, and their famed artillery school, Camp Le Valdahon.

Artillery observation was, and remains, a very precise specialty with little margin for error. Since artillery pieces are positioned behind the front lines, mistakes can mean directing artillery shells onto your own troops. During World War I, short falling shells exploding anywhere near an army's own lines could be especially deadly, as the poison gases used then were most often delivered in artillery shells.

Len would train for his military specialty using primarily four items: a set of 6 power field glasses (binoculars), a civilian compass (military ones would be issued in France) marked in 360 degrees, a plotting board with a military map, and a field phone (service buzzer) for transmitting orally or in Morse code. His classroom instruction included learning the "long" and "short" tones that comprise the dots and dashes ("dits" & "dahs") of Morse code.

The Morse code Len studied included not only the 26 letters of the English alphabet, but also punctuation and the Arabic numerals zero through nine. The military also used a series of "trench codes," or ciphers, taught to appropriate personnel once in France. These were acronyms and abbreviations that were just one to three letters long, and had opposite meanings depending upon whether the signal was being sent from the frontline to the rear or vice versa. Aside from a military compass (marked in mils), another item given to scouts during training in France was an Alidade that served as a map ruler as well as a level and sight.

Len's advanced training began each day with 30 minutes of calisthenics, followed by four hours of classroom instruction in Morse, then 30 minutes for lunch, followed by four hours of land navigation. The land navigation included classroom as well as field training.

The learning of land navigation was essential for a scout who had to know how to use a military map for navigating, and thus, plotting the location of enemy targets as well. Among the American infantry of 1917–18, land navigation was not normally a part of an enlisted man's training since there was thought to be no need for it. The thinking at the time was that men were to be led by officers and NCOs already trained in such things. Besides, what land navigation was needed for a soldier in his trench to "go over the top" and charge an enemy trench a few hundred yards ahead? Germans interrogating American prisoners of war often discovered that most of these men were unable to use or even read a military map. In fact, the shortage of proper military maps required many American infantry officers to use civilian maps; this was still true in WWII when American scouts and tankers were using touring maps of WWI French battlefields produced by Michelin Tire back in 1920.

Artillery fire could not be corrected without communication between the scout and his battery. It was the M1917 field phone, manufactured by Kellogg Switchboard & Supply (in Chicago), that was the most desired form of communication, but it was in short supply as were switchboards. The switchboard shortage was lessened when one was occasionally captured from the Germans.

Scouts usually had to depend on some of the older, yet more plentiful, forms of transmission equipment, like the Signal Corps' battery powered M1914 Service Buzzer. It was a field telegraph with a telegraph key for transmitting in Morse code, and was also a phone with headset and voice mike. The M1914 Service Buzzer was manufactured by Stromberg-Carlson and was a powerful transmitter. Allegedly, it posed a potential security threat as its transmissions could supposedly be picked up by German troops using crystal radio sets. That claim was probably more legend than fact.

Scouts usually were placed in groups of six men and operated in pairs in the field. One man spotted while his partner transmitted the designated position of a target. Len and Al Slowey were normally assigned to form one of these two man teams for Battery A in the 124th Field Artillery Regiment. Also essential to Len's training was how to ride and care for a horse. Scouts in the artillery at that time were expected to move about the front on horseback. This was a primary reason why all the training camps had large remount depots. Horse teams, consisting of six horses per caisson, were also needed to lug the artillery pieces as well as other wagons and equipment to and from the battlefield. Being a city boy from Chicago, Len had no prior experience whatsoever with horses. He was intimidated by their very presence at first, but daily visits to the remount depot for training helped him to quickly overcome his apprehension. He actually started to develop a fondness for the animals.

Horse training for men like Len had to start at the most rudimentary level. Learning how to place a blanket over the animal's back and then secure a saddle to it, as well as how to place a bridle in its mouth, all accomplished while gripped with the fear of being bitten or kicked at any time.

His hands trembled the first time he went to place a bridle on his horse. "Don't worry Fairfield," the NCO remarked. "It's the mules who bite fingers off. They hate people. The horses usually kick you in the head when you least expect it." Len's proficiency with horses was obtained under duress. His fears were somewhat abated as he won his animal's affection with the customary practices of hand feeding it carrot and apple slices as well as the occasional lump of sugar.

Len was assigned a gelding called "Blackie." The first time the animal may have tried to demonstrate its affection in return for Len's very humane treatment, Len was taken by surprise. Blackie went to rub his face on Len's chest, an action that can be a sign of affection from a horse, but Len had no idea what Blackie's intentions were. He panicked and tried in vain to push the animal away. This only resulted in his being knocked to the ground amongst a chorus of laughter from his fellow Doughboys.

Riding techniques were, and remain, basic. To go left, one simply pulls the reins to the left; to go right, one pulls them to the right. At the same time, pressure is applied with the toes to point the horse in the desired direction. If the horse hesitates—not an uncommon behavior for an animal that wants to determine just who is in charge—then one puts some slack in the reins and whips its neck to remind it who its master happens to be. Forward movement was encouraged when the rider banged his heals into the horse's side. Spurs, Model 1874, were used to accomplish the task.

Len and the others were also taught to monitor their horse's health by checking its mouth for any sign of change in color or weak gums, along with its hooves to make certain that its shoes were fitting properly, free of large or sharp debris, and mostly dry. The shoes for a civilian horse would be changed about every eight to ten weeks, but a military horse usually had to be shod in about half, or even a third, of that time.

Most importantly, the horses had to be checked for the "mange." This highly contagious disease effects a horse's (and mule's) skin and can make it dry and cracked to the point where the animal has to be put down. It begins in small areas made obvious by hair loss. If left untreated, it spreads quickly. The treatment at the time was a "dipping vat," a huge vat big enough to allow the animal to be immersed, containing a vile mixture of lime and sulfur that was then brought to a boil. This was a clear case of the cure for the poor animal being as bad or worse than the disease.

During World War I, humans and animals alike both became casualties not only from the customary weapons of war, but from a new and grisly method of killing and maiming—poison gas. Its extensive use, primarily in artillery shells but occasionally in cloud form from canisters, choked, blinded, and destroyed any unprotected living creature in its path. A variety of gases were used: chlorine, phosgene, and mustard (more chemical than gas), or a gruesome cocktail mixture containing a variation of some, or all of the above named agents. These gases acted on bodily fluids and moisture and caused severe blistering and burning both in and outside the body. The gas masks that the soldiers trained so extensively with and wore for protection were crude, primitive, and often less then fully effective.

When gas was known to be present, which was the case during most of the fair sized engagements of WWI, a klaxon ("battle rattle") was immediately sounded. The klaxon was often nothing more than a spent artillery shell hanging from a metal rod, with a nightstick-like piece of wood suspended on a small piece of rope attached to it. In the event of a gas attack, whoever was closest to the klaxon immediately started to bang away on it. This was the signal for every man to put on his gas mask.

In addition to their own gas masks, riders were expected to place a specially designed, "feedbag" like mask over their horse's face. The masks for horses were even less effective than those for humans. The gallows humor amongst the Doughboys was that a horse exposed to poison gas could die in as little as 5 minutes, but if the mask was applied in time, then the horse could survive for a full 5 minutes. "Not to worry," the soldiers further joked amongst themselves, since it normally took about 10 minutes to get the mask on the resistant horse in the first place!

Horses were harder to come by than soldiers. According to author Robert Ferrell in *America's Deadliest Battle*, the shortage of proper shipping meant that Americans could seldom get their own horses transported to France, and often had to purchase second rate ones from the French for as much as $400 a piece (almost $6,600 in 2012 dollars). Doughboys assigned horses were responsible for monitoring their horse's care; missing a condition that caused the animal health problems made for serious trouble for the soldier. Perhaps this was another military example of equipment having a greater priority and value than men.

Len soon learned to examine, saddle, and bridle his horse with speed and efficiency and quickly developed fairly capable riding skills. He could even get a mask on Blackie's face in less than a minute.

He was given a bit of advice that would stay with him always. Even experienced animals, those accustomed to being under fire, can panic, rear up, or bolt. They could charge into no man's land, or in any direction, dragging their thrown riders to their death. For this reason, riders were cautioned not to insert anything beyond the ball of their foot into the stirrups. This way they stood a better chance of jumping or being thrown clear if their horse suddenly bucked.

Len demonstrated proficiency with his duties and on February 19, 1918, he was promoted to Private First Class (Pfc) in the field artillery. He would now sew on his upper sleeve the famed, and prized, cross cannons of a Pfc artilleryman. Having learned about weapons, equipment, and animals, this was about the time that their combat training began in earnest. They were taken into a set of training trenches where British and French instructors, experienced in war, tried to simulate battle conditions as realistically as possible. These included things like live machine gun fire over the heads of trainees as they crawled out from the trenches.

Gas attacks were practiced as well. Tear gas was the agent used for getting the trainees accustomed to gas attacks and provided a very real incentive for applying the mask properly over the face and taking the entire drill seriously. Those who didn't get their gas masks on fast enough, or snug enough, were quick to stand out as they were the ones with burning eyes, vomiting, and facial cavities a gush in mucous.

Len and the others trained with the British small box respirator (SBR). The SBR was a canister gas mask that was one of the more reliable masks at the time. The masks were designed to fit very snugly, but in order for the masks to fit properly a soldier had to have a short haircut and a close shave. Everyone complained that the masks' fogged lenses obstructed vision. They were difficult to breath with and caused a certain degree of claustrophobia. Still, it was the only counter measure to a very deadly weapon, and only a fool didn't have their gas mask readily available in a forward area.

The 124th was not the only artillery regiment of the 33rd Division. There were also the 122nd and 123rd Field Artillery Regiments, along with the 108th Trench Mortar Battery. These units, along with the 108th Supply Train and the 108th Ammunition Train, were brought together to comprise the newly formed 58th Field Artillery Brigade (FAB) under the command of Brigadier General Henry G. Todd, Jr.

This unit was designated to become an elite and highly mobile organization, specializing in close fire support and dealing out hard-hitting punishment to the enemy. Because many artillery units and flying squadrons could be quickly dismantled, moved from one part of the front to another, and then just as quickly re-assembled (much like a traveling civilian circus), they were often referred to as "circus" units—circus artillery, the flying circus, etc.

With the 58th Field Artillery Brigade's designation as a circus unit, the army detached it from the 33rd Infantry Division and gave them an independent status, allowing them to be placed wherever they were needed most. The 58th FAB would provide support to no fewer than four (a fifth unofficially) American infantry divisions during combat in France.

Just as Len had to ready his mind and body for combat, his conscience also needed to be properly prepared. The army could teach him how to find his way in a combat area with a compass and a map, but they could not ease his moral qualms with mere instruction. As a devout Roman Catholic, Len did not see the taking of human life as a trivial duty. His moral compass needed to be as properly aligned as his military one.

First, he had serious misgivings about the war. It seemed like another pointless European rift that didn't really concern Americans. True, a few years prior the Germans had sunk the civilian *Lusitania* and killed approximately 200 Americans in the process, but those Americans had travelled at their own risk, despite warnings from Germany, and Wilson hadn't taken the country to war over the matter.

And while Germany had offered to throw in with Mexico in a war against the United States, any American with half a brain knew that Mexico would never accept such an offer. For the last seven years, Mexico had been in various forms of revolution and civil war and was hardly in a position to go to war with the United States; not to mention that the Mexicans had taken such a beating from the U.S. during the 1846–1848 war over Texas, that no sane person could imagine them wanting to relive an experience like that again. As for unrestricted submarine warfare by Germany, was freedom for a neutral country, like America, to bring war related materials across the sea to Britain really such a necessity? Len, like a lot of religious men, Catholic, Jewish, and Protestant alike, had serious moral reservations about America's participation in this war. Moral reluctance to kill over such matters was not limited to Alvin York or even solely to military personnel. Wilson's government, however, was more than prepared for this scenario.

Wilson quickly established the Committee on Public Information

Zoom out to larger picture [handwritten annotation]

(CPI) headed by George Creel, a Mississippi newspaper editor and almost fanatical supporter of Wilson and the war effort. Creel established his own army of 75,000 volunteers to address public gatherings in support of the war. They were told to limit their speeches to no more than four minutes in length and for this reason they were quickly dubbed the "Four Minute Men." Creel's volunteer army showed up all across the United States and spoke at movie houses, social, charitable, and political events, churches, synagogues, and seemingly anywhere else where people might gather. Creel claimed that over seven million four-minute speeches were delivered to enough people to cover the population of the United States twice over.

In regards to the Catholic and Protestant clergy, military service was seen as a way for "real men" to emulate the life of Christ. Military life required sacrifice, courage, devotion to duty, putting others' needs ahead of one's own, and a willingness to lay down one's very life if necessary.

Giovanni Battista della Chiesa had been elected by the College of Cardinals to the Papacy in September of 1914, a month after the start of the war, and had chosen to become Pope Benedict XV. Giovanni had chosen his papal name after St. Benedict of Nursia who was noted for his love of peace, reason, and later recognized as a patron of Europeans. While Benedict XV referred to the war as the "suicide of civilized Europe," and would even offer a peace plan of his own in August of 1917, one thoroughly rejected by all sides, he never condemned the war as unjust or said that Catholics could not participate in it.

While the American Conference of Catholic Bishops did not yet exist in 1917, the church in America did have an unofficial spokesman and leader. That man was Cardinal James Gibbons of Baltimore, and he issued a public letter in support of America's role in the war. The near unanimous thinking of Catholic clergy in 1917 was that Catholics were not pacifists, had to render unto Caesar that which was due Caesar and, of course, that the German "Huns" were evil. In the words of Saint Paul, a Catholic must wield the sword of Justice in defense of the defenseless—in this case, against Germany and in defense of Belgium, Luxembourg, and parts of occupied France.

These thoughts were widely circulated in publications like "Stars and Stripes," as well as in homilies and the confessionals of priests serving as military chaplains. This allowed Len to point his moral compass in the direction of fulfilling his duties as a soldier in wartime. He might not care for the political, social, or historical bearings behind the conflict, but he could perform his duties with a relatively clear conscience.

After roughly six months at Camp Logan, most of the men in the 58th FAB felt ready, willing, and eager, even if rather short of able, to join the enemy in battle. The army was desperate to get as many men to France as quickly as possible, and was all too happy to oblige the men's enthusiasm. The 33rd Infantry Division was beefed up with the addition of 7,000 new recruits in April. Orders came down in early May for them to head "over there" to the Western Front. The 33rd Division was to depart Camp Logan for Camp Merritt in Tenafly, New Jersey on May 14th for a brief period before shipping out to Europe. Len was able to get off a telegram with this info to Maggie before his unit departed from Houston.

It was at Camp Logan in 1918 that the insignia for the 33rd Division was created. Their equipment had to be designated as their own before leaving for France. Illinois volunteers serving in the Philippines during the Spanish-American War and subsequent insurrection had learned that the locals there were superstitious about yellow crosses, so they took to painting them on their equipment to mark ownership. It seemed like an appropriate practice to continue.

Len now received two new pieces of equipment from the army. Artillery rounds had to be carefully timed in coordination with attacks. For this reason, he was issued an Ingersoll wristwatch. Until the First World War, men carried pocket watches, which were not practical for use in the trenches. The Ingersoll Company earned recognition and success for their mass production of the dollar pocket watch. Their advertising slogan was, "the watch that made the dollar famous." Their first wristwatches produced for the American military were nothing more than one of their pocket watches, minus a cover, mounted with wire lugs atop a wristband. Wristwatches, or "wristlettes," as they were known then, were women's wear. The circumstances of the Great War would forever change that.

Len was also issued a set of "dog tags." In World War I these were round aluminum, about the size of a half dollar, with the soldier's name, rank, unit, and "USA" stamped on the front and the soldier's serial number stamped on the back. Len's serial number was 1-378-723. Dog tags were suspended around the neck with either white canvas strips or thin leather straps. Everyone knew its purpose. In the event of death, one tag was left on the soldier's body for Grave's Registration to properly identify their body while the second was turned over to their commanding officers for record of their death and to notify the next of kin.

There was no mistaking now that this was really war and that war's intended and primary consequence is to deliver death. They all knew that some of them would not be coming back, and a nervous shiver ran through Len as he placed the set of cold disks and leather strap around his neck. In just a few months the 58th FAB would be very much in the thick of things and a very real player in the big show.

CHAPTER 3

The Yanks Are Coming
to be Buried Over Here

L EN AND THE REST of the 124th Field Artillery left Camp Logan on May 14, 1918 and boarded Pullman cars bound for Camp Merritt in Cresskill, New Jersey. Prior to departing, Len had telegrammed his new bride that he was being sent there before his unit would ship out for France. Maggie wasted no time and immediately arranged for a week off from her Western Union job and train passage to the coast.

Camp Merritt was initially named Camp Tenafly. Tenafly, New Jersey was the city in which the camp was designed, and acted as the administrative oversight area for its construction. Most people mistakenly thought that was also where the camp was located. After her train arrived in New Jersey, Maggie took a cab to Tenafly only to learn immediately after it dropped her off that she was still a few miles south of Camp Merritt. Fortunately, nearby there was a small depot with an empty bus standing idle and some soldiers milling about. Maggie inquired of the bus driver if one of his destinations was Camp Merritt. "M'am, that's my only destination," the driver replied. "The fare's a dollar and just as soon as I have 12 paid customers, I'll be on my way."

Maggie was busting at the seams to see Len and excitedly offered to charter the entire bus herself. That was fine with the driver. If she was willing to pay for the bus, he was willing to take her as its sole passenger. Maggie couldn't help but notice all of the soldiers who were sitting and milling about the depot with long faces. She asked the driver why they were there and looking so down trodden.

"They spent their leave time and their money in town," the driver answered. "Now they're putting off the walk back to camp for as long as they can."

Fate was smiling on everyone that day. There were eighteen soldiers present and Maggie wasn't going to turn a single one away. She opened up her purse, counted out $19.00 to cover her fare and that of the impoverished Doughboys. She gave it to the driver who promptly blew his horn and waived everyone aboard. The overjoyed soldiers scrambled onto the bus, continuously thanking her as the epitome of kindness and asking if there was anything they could do to return the favor to this most gracious of souls. "Well," Maggie said. "There is in fact something you can help me with."

"Anything! Anything!" They assured her. All she had to do was name it. She explained her mission and asked them if they could locate Len once they got to camp. The Doughboys would be only too happy to oblige and said that all they needed was her husband's name and unit, which Maggie gladly provided. Their help was essential, as Camp Merritt covered almost 800 acres and had more than 40,000 soldiers stationed there.

Shortly after their arrival, Maggie was escorted to an office at the camp's entrance, as security regulations specifically prohibited civilians from any other access into the camp. The Doughboys asked her to have a seat and wait. She didn't have to wait too long as the grateful soldiers soon returned in a mock honor guard procession triumphantly escorting an overjoyed Len to his lovely wife and their angel of mercy.

The couple wanted to spend some time alone together, but Len had no pass or ability to acquire one at the moment so they did the only thing possible under the circumstances—Len slipped out the front gate and went AWOL to spend a little time with his bride in Hoboken. In addition to her return trip train ticket, and money set aside to pay for a hotel stay, Maggie had $52.00 in cash and even a fraction of that could buy a near-gourmet dinner in 1918. The newlyweds enjoyed steaks, baked potatoes, and asparagus, with a common but still tasty red wine. This of course was followed by a romantic, if not hasty, interlude in Maggie's hotel room.

It would be thirteen months before the couple would see each other again. They didn't decide on it at the time, but they came to regard "Till We Meet Again" as their song; at least in regards to the war.

The guards posted at Camp Merritt's gate, as well as Len's barracks chief, turned a blind eye and a deaf ear to his rather late and somewhat unorthodox return. He was never listed as being AWOL.

There was a final round of physical exams at the camp to weed out anybody who may have had a disqualifying condition that was previously missed, or those who had suspected symptoms of flu. Len was half hoping they might find some reason to hold him back but it was not to be.

The men were issued their remaining equipment including gas masks and head protection. Their helmets were "saucepan" styled, identical to the British design, and the Doughboys referred to them as "tin hats." The helmets did not have their division's insignia painted on the front. In fact, none of the AEF's helmets had insignia on them. With the rare exception of chaplains, who sometimes painted crosses, angel wings, and other religious symbols on their helmets, the Doughboys would not get around to painting any insignia on their helmets until their desire to find something to do during the extreme boredom of post war occupation.

Len was relieved that since his military specialty required him to ride horses, he would not be wearing the miserable 1918 issue trench boots, but instead the 1910 hobnail rider's boots which did not have the seemingly unbendable triple soles that the infantry had to tolerate.

Orders were received on May 26th for the 58th Field Artillery Brigade to embark the following day at the port of Hoboken for transport to Europe. The morning came early and started without breakfast, the sergeants barking out orders to "Gear up and fall in!" as the men scrambled to comply. Trains provided quick transport to Hoboken where security was tight. The portion of the city near the docks had been under martial law for some time, and several of the city's German immigrants, considered "enemy aliens," had been forcibly evicted from the city.

The ship that would transport Len and the other men of the 124th Field Artillery was the *Melita*. The *Melita* was a Canadian Pacific transport, which had been converted to military use. Other troop ships transporting the units of the 58th FAB were the *Kashmir*, the *Scotian*, and the

City of Poona. General Todd and his staff would sail a few days later on the *Mauretani.*

As Len boarded the ship, he and the others were presented with a colored tag to pin on their uniform. This was a necessity since the men were rapidly herded like cattle onto a ship that was seriously over capacity. Roughly five thousand men were jammed onto a "troop" ship designed to carry only half that number. These overcrowded conditions necessitated everything being done in shifts. The tag determined a soldier's shift for sleeping as well as eating. It also designated where he was to sleep and even his station area for abandoning ship in the event they were torpedoed by a German submarine.

As the *Melita* disembarked from the port at Hoboken to sail up the Hudson River and into the Atlantic, the soldiers on board broke out into song: "Good-bye Broadway, Hello France!" General John J. Pershing, Commander of the American Expeditionary Force (AEF), had promised America's soldiers a speedy end to the war in 1917, and boldly proclaimed that they'd be in "Heaven, Hell or Hoboken by Christmas." Obviously, the war had not ended with the troops returning home, via the port at Hoboken, by Christmas of 1917; in fact, the United States wouldn't even have enough men in France for a meaningful engagement of their own until May of 1918 (Cantigny). But at this moment in 1918, the Doughboys had high hopes of fulfilling Pershing's battle cry.

The *Melita* and her sister ships were a convoy of four. "Submarine Chasers" (British destroyers) would rendezvous with them, if German submarines were thought to be active, once the convoy entered the waters off Ireland. German submarines at the time could not operate effectively off the American coast because of the distance from their home ports (a problem technology would solve by the next world war) so destroyer escorts were not normally necessary until American transports came within miles of the shores of either the United Kingdom or France. Troop ships moved continuously in a zigzag pattern during the entire journey across the Atlantic to make them more difficult targets for potential enemy torpedoes.

Men were fed a generally miserable quality of food and in groups of a thousand at a time. The hardtack, however, was British and more edible than its American counterpart. In the words of one doughboy, it was "more like a biscuit of 'Shredded Wheat' and could actually be chewed." In the morning, the braver souls ate the regular servings of eggs. It took real courage, as the eggs were hard boiled, served in the shell, and kept in cold storage. Many a doughboy bit into a fairly well formed chicken as opposed to a soft yoke. The stewed rabbits served at dinner were less than appetizing and referred to by the men as "stewed cats."

The soldiers ate, emesis aside, not only standing but in continuous motion. As he entered the mess area, chow ("slop") was dumped into Len's, and the other Doughboys' mess kits as they moved along in single file. They ate as they walked, or in some instances slid, through the puddles of vomit on the floor, toward the exit. The tables were bolted to the floor but had no seats. They had no pragmatic function among so large a group.

The "troop ships" were converted almost entirely from commercial vessels—passenger and cargo. Private owners rather than naval authorities operated them and they usually exploited soldiers to the fullest. The canteens on board might offer candy or fruits, but at three, four, or even five times the normal price. Few could afford to indulge themselves.

The seas were generally calm, and because of that and the severe overcrowding, men were allowed on deck. Seasickness was a common occurrence and many a Doughboy hung over the rail of a swaying ship, "feeding the fish," as he must have wondered if combat wasn't preferable to his current agony. Len puzzled at how it was possible for a vessel to seemingly rock back and forth while simultaneously moving up and down. He didn't have long to ponder this question, as he had to take his occasional turn hanging over the rail "feeding the fish."

Since the men slept in shifts, the bunks were always "hot" from the body heat of the man who vacated it just seconds before its next scheduled occupant took possession. Some of the bunks were hammocks while others were wooden frames bolted to the wall with a wire bottom. The only "mattress" in such a situation was a blanket thrown over the wires.

The ships were blacked out at night as a security measure against submarine attack. There were many drills requiring the men to assemble at their assigned station for abandoning ship. The abandon ship stations assigned to the troops were portals to death. In the event the ship was torpedoed, the soldiers were to put on their coats, gloves, and life jackets. The life jackets were sarcastically referred to by the men as "sinkers"—they were filled with cork that quickly water-logged, transforming them from flotation devices into weights. Then they were to jump into the cold Atlantic before climbing into a raft or lifeboat. This was probably the only procedure possible under the circumstances, but hardly one likely to enhance survival.

When on deck and not seasick, Len was impressed with the view as well as the sense of reality that was beginning to sink in. They really were heading "over there." He was on his way to the battlefields of France.

The *Melita*'s final destination was the same as many American troop ships—Liverpool. It arrived on the 8th of June. The ships entered up through the Mersey River and were escorted to the docks by tugs. As many soldiers as possible squeezed and wormed their way onto the deck. Len was no exception. He was glad the journey was over and even his cynical side was suppressed by the sounds of cheering crowds. The city had no banners or flags but there were plenty of British civilians on hand, and both soldiers and the spectators on the shore waved and cheered one another with great enthusiasm.

As the gangplanks were put into place, the Doughboys prepared to disembark in full uniform with all their equipment and belongings. Len stepped from the gangplank onto the dock and one of the civilian spectators, obviously drunk, pointed at the haversack up on his back and asked, "Hey Yank, what's 'at up 'ere on your back?" Len was stunned at the stupidity of the question and couldn't resist a snappy answer. Without skipping a beat, he replied, "Bunker Hill, ya damned fool!"

Len and the others marched through the streets of Liverpool toward Camp Knotty Ash some six miles away. It was a rest camp designed to quarter its occupants for a period lasting no more than a day or two. As they moved along Liverpool's streets, people, especially children, reached out to touch them, hand out flowers, cigarettes, tea, and occasionally even kiss the soldiers as they passed along through the crowds. There was a real jubilation in the air as if salvation had arrived. Shouts of "Welcome Yanks!" and "Hey Sammies!" echoed along the entire route. The term "Sammies" was used as a reference to American soldiers by the French and British. It was detested by the Doughboys and never stuck with Americans.

The title of "Sammies" was obviously referring to the Americans as sons of Uncle Sam. But just where the term "Doughboy" originated cannot be answered with certainty. U.S. soldiers who fought Apache Indians in the American Southwest, Spanish in Cuba, and insurgents in the Philippines, fought in hot dusty climates. The soldiers were drenched in sweat and often covered with dust. This gave their faces a dough-like appearance and that is the most generally accepted origin of the term "Doughboy."

Still, some claim the term came from the fact that American soldiers were paid more money (dough) than their British and French counterparts. Finally, others said the American haversacks resembled blobs of dough and this gave birth to the term. Whatever the reason, it was "Doughboys" that Americans, soldiers and civilians alike, adopted as the official term for the nation's fighting men.

IN THE FIRST HALF of the 20th century, "Doughboy" was a term to Americans that came to signify one tough hombre.

As the soldiers marched along, Len's eyes rolled as many in the ranks took up the chorus of "Over There'" yet again. At 25, he was no longer a naïve kid and was never gripped by war fever. He didn't consider this a great adventure, rite of passage, or noble crusade. He knew this was serious business and the stakes were life and death.

Since the time when the boat disembarked from New Jersey, the soldiers had only one song that rivaled the constant repetition of "Over There," and that was "Hail, Hail the Gang's All Here." That was a song Len liked and he joined in with gusto. He hoped and prayed that as many of the gang as possible, himself foremost, would be around to sing it again when it was time to return home.

At the train station the Red Cross had arranged for the soldiers to receive hot coffee, cookies, and that most fattening of American comfort foods—"doughnuts." These rings of dough, fried, or boiled in hot grease and sprinkled with powdered sugar were a delicacy beyond description.

As Len and his compatriots marched through the streets of Liverpool munching donuts, they were handed a flier with a message from the king. It read:

Windsor Castle

Soldiers of the United States, the people of the British Isles welcome you on your way to take your stand beside the Armies of many Nations now fighting in the Old World the great battle for human freedom.

The Allies will gain new heart & spirit in your company.

I wish that I could shake the hand of each one of you & bid you God speed on your mission.

(signed) George R. I.

His Majesty King George V

April 1918

Len was somewhat less than impressed and without regard stuffed it into his pocket. Some used it to supplement their toilet paper supply but it seemed most saved it for souvenir purposes.

Marches for the Doughboys, especially on paved or stone streets, were no easy task. Most of Len's comrades were wearing the new 1918 trench boot that had not one, not two, but three leather soles that were sewn and further bound together with hobnails. Add some heel plates and half toed iron cleats and one can appreciate why the Doughboys referred to them as "little tanks." They did a very good job of protecting the wearer's foot but made it near impossible for him to bend it. On smooth and slippery surfaces like floors or cobblestones, the soldiers "rocked" more than walked. As many a doughboy said, "it was one step forward and two backwards."

Knotty Ash was mostly a tent city with a hospital. It provided the men an opportunity to rest, but not to fill their aching stomachs since there was little to eat. Here, the idea was to give men a chance to relax, maybe bathe or do laundry, write letters, and play some American football. These were all good intentions but far from the reality of what the camp actually provided.

The respite at Knotty Ash was brief; a mere day. With their time for recuperation over, the Doughboys were aroused at 5:30 am, fed, and then ordered to fall out with their gear for a rail ride to Winchester. From Winchester, they marched to Camp Wendell Downs, another "rest camp" where, once again, they received only a single day's rest. They then boarded a train for Southampton. This meant embarkation for Le Havre, France. Like Liverpool, Southampton civilians turned out to welcome and cheer their new allies. Len couldn't help but think how easy it was for the civilians to cheer—after all, they weren't going anywhere.

The Doughboys boarded English cattle boats to cross the channel. The journey was only 130 miles and took some five to six hours. Not enough time for Len to get seasick or to rest but enough time to reflect on all that was happening and to worry some. The soldiers reached Le Havre at about 4:30 in the morning, but were not allowed to disembark until mid-afternoon when the tide made movements more accommodating.

Things were moving very rapidly now. A month earlier, Len and his outfit were in Hoboken. They had since crossed the Atlantic, traversed England, crossed the Channel and soon the men of the 124th Field Artillery would be setting foot on French soil.

The arrival at Le Havre was nothing like Liverpool. There were no civilians, cheering or otherwise. Len and the others were ordered to disembark quickly and form up into ranks. Len could feel a knot form in his stomach as if he and his comrades were about to march directly into battle. Instead, their march was a five-mile trek to an Army processing center known as Camp Le Havre.

Their stay there was short. The unit and its members were accounted for, and Len's commanders received their orders. They were to march another three miles into Le Havre proper where they would board trains at the station and proceed to Ornans to be billeted and receive additional classroom instruction. They would then depart for the French artillery school at nearby Camp Le Valdahon. It was, after all, the French under Napoleon Bonaparte who truly developed artillery into a highly useful battlefield weapon. Who better than the French to complete the Americans' training in such a deadly art?

During all the major conflicts of the 20th Century, artillery fire has been responsible for the greatest percentage of combat related deaths and wounds. Contrary to popular thought, only about one percent of the soldiers in World War I were killed by poison gas and about the same percentage with bayonets. Artillery was without doubt the king of battle.

With the processing of the 124th Field Artillery completed, the men were ordered to fall in for the march to the train station in Le Havre. There were rail (box) cars for their transportation. The cars were only twenty-and-a-half feet long and eight-and-a-half feet wide, about half the size of an American boxcar.

Scrawled on the side of each boxcar was "40 hommes et 8 chevaux": 40 men and 8 horses, better known as the famed "forty–and–eights" of the First World War. The cars were seldom, if ever, cleaned beyond basic sweeping and there were no shortages of bugs, vermin, dirty straw, fecal remnants, and bad smells. Once loaded aboard, the men were so cramped that they knew there could never be any room for horses. These cars hauled either 40 men or 8 horses but never both together. Obviously, the floor of the car revealed its previous cargo had been equine.

The officers were boarded on the train's few coach cars. Len couldn't help but feel a pang of resentment at the obvious example of rank having its privileges.

Len and the others were handed a "traveling ration" as they boarded their assigned boxcar. The ration consisted of canned corned beef ("willy"), canned tomatoes, and what Union soldiers of the American Civil War referred to as "hard crackers" (hardtack). This more modern version of an age-old military ration had the crackers conveniently pre-soaked by issuing them in a tin filled with water. In theory, they'd be softened and thus edible.

"Eat it all, men!" some hard-nosed sergeant barked out. "You don't know when you'll get more and be glad this isn't like the hardtack you'd normally get." In fact, the hard crackers, while packed in water, were as solid as concrete. A few trusting souls tried to gnaw on them, while some anonymous wag in the back of the car echoed everyone's sentiment when he used a cracker to tap out "B.S." on the floor in Morse code. The sergeant looked up wondering whether or not he had heard something. Len and the others chuckled in muffled tones at the phantom's action.

The distance from Le Havre to Ornans is close to 400 miles and would require almost two days by slow moving rail to get there. The army intended to make the journey as rapidly as possible with the fewest number of stops necessary for stretching, issuing rations, and the necessities of nature.

The train's route was well to the west of the battlefront, with its final destination in the French Province of Franche-Comté along the Swiss bor-

thrice!

der so the journey could be made in relative safety and without incident. This was late June and the peace and tranquility of the French countryside was matched only by *its* beauty. Len may have been raised in urban Chicago but had made occasional excursions to the "country," and the train's brief stops along the French countryside provided a comforting feeling and reminder of things back home.

Len wondered how Maggie was doing back there. He knew the army censors carefully screened the mail. Once they were at Ornans, they would be assigned an army post office (APO) number, which would be the only address Maggie would have for writing him. In return, the only clue to his own location that Len would be able to provide Maggie would be to use the approved phrase, "Somewhere in France."

The train's arrival in Ornans couldn't have been more welcomed by the Doughboys. Cramped quarters, two days of sitting and sleeping on the floor of a disgusting boxcar, complimented by the consumption of travel rations, had definitely taken their toll.

Camp Le Valdahon was near the city of the same name some 16 kilometers (10 miles) away from Ornans. It was without doubt the most capable training school for artillerymen in all of France. With the American 5th Field Artillery Brigade having just started their four week training program there, and the school only able to accommodate a single American artillery unit at a time, Len and the other men in his unit would continue their classroom training in Ornans.

Their study would primarily be in learning the trench ciphers regarding the control of artillery fire. They also received a vigorous course of instruction, using French equipment, in plotting targets. It was far more intensive than anything they had had during their time at Camp Logan.

As combat was drawing closer, the men of the 58th FAB were being driven ever harder. They would need to be. Once they completed their final training at Valdahon, they would be deployed quickly to the front where they would be in the thick of the fighting, seeing almost continuous action that would last right up until the very minute that the armistice took effect.

Two postcards from Camp Le Valdahon, where Len did training in France.
Valdahon is the French version of Fort Sill (artillery school) in Oklahoma.

CHAPTER 4

Camp Le Valdahon: Getting a French Education in Survival

T HE FRENCH REGION OF Franche-Comté was untouched by the war. Abutting the Swiss border, it was well removed to the south of the trenches and their associated artillery. Even today it contains some of the country's most beautiful rolling hills and lush landscapes. Len saw this as a much-deserved opportunity for rest after the drudgery of basic training, traversing the Atlantic, and their lateral movements across Britain and then France.

Ornans, a small and pleasant commune with a population of about 2,500 people then, was the area where they would be billeted and given further classroom training while they waited their turn for ever more rigorous artillery training at Camp Le Valdahon. The artillery school at Valdahon was at the time being utilized by the American 5th Artillery Brigade and that was just fine with Len and the others. They could have it for as long as they needed it. Any break from the normal military routine, especially in so beautiful a location, was more than welcome.

Ornans is the birthplace of French painter Gustave Courbet, who created the famed *Burial at Ornans* depicting the burial of his great uncle in 1848. The people of Ornans were pleasant and glad to see their new American allies. Like all the communes surrounding Valdahon, they were long since accustomed to the coming and going of military personnel. While fighting had not come to Ornans, the flu pandemic of 1918 had. It was beginning to infect soldier and civilian alike. It was in fact all through the region including Valdahon. There was little one could do other than to avoid those already infected, practice personal hygiene, and pray. Len diligently performed all three.

As Len had already learned, most American soldiers in 1917–18 received only the most rudimentary military instruction during their basic training in the United States. The drastic need for fresh troops on the Western Front had necessitated that the Doughboys be shipped to Europe as soon as possible. The U.S. had declared war in April of 1917 but it was a full 13 months before there was any meaningful number of combat ready troops in France. The United States would eventually raise an army of four million men, with half of them actually getting to France. The U.S. objective was to churn out recruits with their basic military training being done in America, hustle them rapidly over to France, and then, after arrival, to provide them with advanced battle training in AEF schools related to their assigned specialty.

The Americans established 21 training areas with special schools in Northeastern France, well behind the front lines. The schools covered everything from infantry tactics and communication to combat engineering and aviation. The courses were initially intended to last for as long as four months but the ever growing need for manpower, and the pragmatics of training for the varying specialties, more often than not, reduced the training periods to a mere two to seven weeks in length.

The one exception to the AEF's training structure was their area for field artillery. The American Second Corps Artillery School was located at Camp Le Valdahon about a mile west of the City of Valdahon. Like Ornans, it was near the Swiss border in the Franche-Comté Region. Unlike the other training sectors established for Americans, Valdahon was a permanent French military facility and while the Doughboys there remained under American command, the school's instructors were French officers, most of whom had extensive combat experience. The schools not only provided the opportunity for raw recruits to learn much from the experience of seasoned veterans but also provided a needed respite from battle for those assigned to teach.

Valdahon trained their students in many deadly arts. In addition to artillery, the list of specialties included tanks, combat engineering, and aerial observers who conducted their job suspended in wicker baskets from enormous hydrogen filled balloons called "Sausages." All of these were considered elite corps and the work was very dangerous.

The tanks of the First World War were slow moving, most having a maximum speed of only four miles per hour. This made them especially vulnerable to enemy artillery. Their thin armor could be easily pierced by machine gun and rifle rounds designed to go through them, and they were also very poorly ventilated. Carbon monoxide poisoning from the engine's exhaust was a very real danger. Engineers had to build and maintain trenches and bridges, as well as plant their own land mines and remove whatever land mines the enemy planted. Their work was always done under the watchful eye of enemy machine gunners and snipers.

Those in balloon observation monitored enemy positions from inside a wicker basket suspended by tethers from an observation balloon filled with highly flammable hydrogen. The observer was generally some two thousand feet above the front, equipped with a pair of binoculars, long-range camera, and a wireless for communication. From his position he could record and report any enemy movements along the front.

These balloons were used by both sides and were attacked by each other's airplanes. The planes were often armed with incendiary bullets, or crude rockets, to help ignite the balloon. The pilots flying such missions usually carried written orders from their squadron commanders authorizing their use of incendiaries, since these types of bullets were specifically designed for use against balloons.

With the planes of that era being made of canvas and wood, incendiaries could easily ignite them. The pilots did not wear parachutes because their commanders did not want them abandoning their planes at the first sign of trouble, so it was considered quite a dirty tactic to use incendiaries against an opposing plane—a pilot whose plane was hit by an incendiary would have to decide whether to ride the burning hulk all the way down, or jump to his death. Small wonder that many pilots carried revolvers to shoot themselves in the head in just such an emergency. A pilot captured in a plane armed with incendiaries, but without written orders to attack a balloon, could be subject to summary execution.

Attacking balloons was dangerous, as they were protected not only by their own side's fighter planes but with anti-aircraft guns on the ground. As enemy planes approached to attack, the observer would signal the crew below to start cranking the cable to reel in the balloon. If it appeared that the planes would ignite the balloon before it could be reeled in, the observer, equipped with a parachute, would jump from the basket to his comrades below. An especially dangerous job to be sure.

But above and beyond all the special training previously mentioned, Valdahon was noted for its school of artillery. Originally intended to be open only during the summer months as an artillery school, its utilization expanded with the Great War to all year round and to include a range of military specialties. No military facility in all of France, perhaps even the world, could even hope to offer the kind of training in artillery usage as Valdahon did in 1917–18. The only problem was that the teaching techniques of the French at Valdahon were intended for the static conditions of trench warfare, accepted as the norm by the instructors of the day, and not the type of rapid mobile warfare that Pershing and the rest of the AEF leadership now desired.

While the nearby City of Valdahon is the birthplace of Victor Hugo, the establishment of the military camp in 1907 soon gave the area its most famous distinction. Camp Le Valdahon was then about a mile long and a half-mile wide, located on a summit with an elevation of about 150 feet in the foothills of the Jura Mountains. Its barracks were made of stone and brick and had electric lights. The camp had its own water supply and the officers' barracks even had a dozen flush toilets! The main problem was with the camp's sewage system; it drew in not only human waste but also scraps from the kitchen and even rainwater from the camp's streets. While not a major problem for Valdahon when used as originally intended, such a system was easily overwhelmed with the camp's expanded and year round uses, and flies, especially around the kitchen where the soldiers' latrines were located, were a constant problem.

Camp Valdahon's mess halls were wooden and served not only edible but sometimes even delicious food. A frequent meal was slumgullion, a stew usually containing meat and potatoes. When it was of poor quality, watery with little or no meat, it was simply called "slum," and was more like the food served from rolling kitchens in the field. The better quality of food served at Camp Valdahon was appreciated by the soldiers, but the repetition of the menu was somewhat tiresome. The good conditions at Camp Valdahon reminded Len of Camp Grant back in Rockford.

The artillery range was located at the north end of the camp and was first rate. The equipment, 75mm cannons and 155mm Howitzers, was current, and the camp had some of the most knowledgeable and experienced instructors in the world. The 124th Field Artillery Regiment had begun to take up residence in Camp Le Valdahon on July 27, 1918. It would take about 3 additional days before the entire 58th FAB was situated in the camp. Len could let Maggie know she could write him at APO #704— assuming he'd be around long to receive any of her letters.

What Len didn't know at the time was that Maggie was having a war related adventure of her own back home. She rode the streetcar each day to and from work. A man who regularly rode the same car as Maggie often smiled at her and made polite comments on the weather and other idle matters, and soon they began to have superficial conversations. He was a gentleman and never made anything that could be considered a romantic or sexual advance toward her.

Maggie enjoyed his company on the otherwise dull rides and their conversations became more and more detailed about the goings on in their lives. Although Maggie never mentioned that her husband was in the military, she was taken aback one day when the gentleman boasted rather proudly how he had intentionally avoided registering for the national draft. As if to add insult to injury, he added that he had every intention of laying low until the war was safely over and the danger passed. It was an unusual act of candor, as draft dodgers were know as "slackers" and such action was not only considered unpatriotic but unmanly.

This bothered Maggie greatly and when she got home she asked Mae what, if anything, she should do about. "Your husband is over there likely to get his fool head shot off, while this 'slacker' goes about his merry way," Mae said. "Turn him in for heaven's sake!" Maggie went to the police and they arranged to have some plain-clothes men pick him up as he exited the streetcar on a predetermined morning. Everything would be done discreetly and this man would never know that Maggie played any role in his capture.

On the big day, Maggie boarded the streetcar with a rapidly beating heart. A short time later, the man boarded, the two smiled at one another, and he took his customary seat next to her. Maggie greeted him with her usual pleasantries and the two immediately began to talk. When they reached his stop, Maggie saw the two plain-clothes officers, wearing "skimmer" hats as a prearranged signal, standing on the corner seemingly engaged in casual conversation. Their target stood up and bid Maggie good day as he headed toward the streetcar's exit.

Maggie turned to the two officers, nodded in the man's direction and watched as the authorities, one displaying a badge, took him by his arms as he stepped from the car. Maggie turned away as if she knew nothing of what had just happened and continued her ride to work.

She never heard another word about the matter or the man involved, but she felt a real sense of accomplishment and satisfaction as if she had personally struck a blow against the forces and circumstances opposing her Len. She had just made a real contribution to the war effort. She knew Len would be proud of her, but she thought it best not to distract him from his duties and responsibilities with any added worry or frustration. She didn't tell him until after he was safely home in 1919.

To be sure, soon after the 124th's arrival at Camp Valdahon, Len and his compatriots quickly realized that this French-run operation was a definite improvement over the conditions to which they had become accustomed. Doughboys in training were generally regarded by the American and British officers over them as ignoramuses. They were constantly reminded of all they didn't know and of the Herculean efforts their superiors had to exert just to try and get them up to the most rudimentary levels of performance.

The French, on the other hand, treated these young and inexperienced American troops, almost all of whom had less than a year of military service, as students who had come to learn. The Doughboys were not barked and screamed at—being treated as raw recruits—but instead were treated more like gentlemen on a college campus. The instructors were there to teach "an art" and not merely program a military automaton.

The ever-increasing need for Allied bodies on the frontlines meant that the training courses were becoming shorter by the calendar and longer by the day. The artillery range at Valdahon was in use from 7:00 in the morning until noon every day but Sunday. Afternoons were spent on the range or in classrooms learning artillery theories and application.

Starting on Saturday night, a bus would transport Doughboys the 26 kilometers (17 miles) from Valdahon to Besançon, the capital and most prominent city in the Franche-Comté region. It was just the prescription necessary after six days of intense training. Len, never one to miss mass on Sunday, attended Catholic liturgies in Besançon.

Flu seemed to be pursuing Len personally in 1918, and cases in his regiment continued to rise. During Len's three-and-a-half weeks at Camp Le Valdahon, some 6.5%, or roughly 200 men from the 58th FAB would have to be admitted to the camp Hospital #12 for influenza, with Battery E of the 124th being especially hard hit. They had some 16% of their men who contracted the life-threatening flu while at Valdahon.

Hospital #12 consisted of three stone buildings and had a bed capacity for 300, but almost as soon as the 58th FAB departed, and the 6th Brigade took their place, it would be overwhelmed with flu cases resulting in even the camp's YMCA facilities being converted into a makeshift hospital.

The Surgeon General's office ordered sanitation squads to thoroughly investigate the matter and inspect the camp while Len and his unit were still there. They concluded that the flu cases were due primarily to the intermingling with civilians in the nearby towns and the "filthy" conditions in the barracks. French and American command at the school disagreed with the latter conclusion, but the barracks were scrubbed after the 58th's departure in late August—although events seem to demonstrate it did little good. As the investigation drew to a close, there was even consideration of moving the 58th FAB to another area to complete their training, but since they were scheduled to depart in a matter of days anyway, it was decided to have them remain in place. It would be the subsequent unit's worry.

———————

THE ARTILLERY BARRAGES and bombardments of the First World War almost always proceeded major assaults and were meant primarily to destroy barbed wire defenses and reduce enemy strong points before the infantry charged across no man's land and into the enemy's trenches. They pulverized and scarred the landscape as they continually unearthed and reburied the military's dead. Much of the Western Front resembled a moonscape. It was said that during the ten-month long Battle of Verdun in 1916, the land was so churned up and devoid of anything above its surface that a soldier could not maintain his sense of direction by mere visual landmarks.

The artillery regiments of the 58th Field Artillery Brigade had each been designated specific types of field guns for training and eventual use. The United States had few artillery pieces of its own and even fewer boats to get them over on (only about 100 American artillery pieces actually got to France) so Americans adopted French field guns for their artillery units. In regards to the 58th FAB, the 122nd and Len's 124th Regiment were assigned to use the famed "French 75" (75mm) as their standard field artillery piece while the 123rd would handle the 155mm Howitzers. The 108th would be a Trench Mortar Battery. The "Trains" of headquarters, military police, ammunition, supply, engineers, and sanitation (military euphemism for ambulances and field hospitals) were all designated as the 108th Trains.

The French had suffered a humiliating defeat at the hands of the Prussians (Germans) during the Franco-Prussian War of 1870, another in the near continuous line of European conflicts. The French were determined after this defeat to develop the best field artillery piece in the world, and between 1894 and 1897 appeared to do just that with the introduction of their 75mm gun.

Dubbed by other nations as the "French 75" it had pragmatic features and an ease of use that was still proficient in 1918 but hardly superior to its counterparts in either Allied or enemy ranks. Its effectiveness was limited largely against enemy personnel rather than their fixed earthworks. Destroying earthworks was a job best left to the more powerful howitzers.

According to Author Ian Hogg, by 1918, the British, Germans, and even Americans had better field pieces, and the French 75 was, and remains today, an overrated field gun whose enhanced reputation has thrived and survived due to its introductory laurels and the insistence of French and American military historians (Americans were issued nearly 4,000 French 75s) to continue to praise the gun their units used.

The exaggerated reputation of the 75's power even spilled into the popular culture of the day. The "French 75" cocktail, or "Soixante-Quinze" in

Soixante-Quinze — caps flims

French, (gin, champagne, lemon juice, and sugar) was named after the field gun. Allied troops on the Western Front often referred to this weapon as the "Soixante-Quinze." It is still held in higher regard than it deserves, but as is often said, "history is written by the victors."

Perhaps the ease of use and ability for rapid fire gave the 75 more reason for praise than its power. Up until the introduction of the French 75, artillery pieces jumped wildly from the recoil following their discharge. This meant that artillery crews had to move their guns back into position and re-aim them again at their intended targets after every round fired, an exhausting and time consuming process. It was also an inefficiency that could prove to be deadly by providing an enemy the opportunity of zeroing in on a battery's position and wiping it out during an artillery duel.

The French 75 changed all this. It used a hydro-pneumatic recoil system accompanied by a form of "anchor" or "brake." This combination allowed the gun's carriage to absorb the recoil while the brake or "earth spade" held the gun in its original place. Without the hydro-pneumatic system to absorb the gun's recoil, an anchor or break would serve only to force the gun to flip itself upside down after being fired.

Gun crews using this new technology had a field piece that could be loaded and discharged rapidly while remaining in place. This allowed for a concentrated and steady stream of artillery fire to be brought down on a specified area. This provided a truly deadly effect on advancing or exposed infantry. Finally, the gun had a system for automatically setting the timing device on an artillery shell whether it was a high explosive (HE) or a shrapnel shell. This would be the gun for which Len would be trained to observe (spot) for and direct (adjust) its fire.

Prior to the First World War, most artillery provided essentially rifle fire at a target that was clearly visible. This meant that a cannon could fire a round in a straight line at a target it could see. Artillery firing of this nature is referred to as "direct fire." This is known as "laying" into the enemy.

During the American Civil War, trench mortars allowed artillery to be fired at an exceptionally steep angle enabling a shell to arch and land on an unseen target, like an enemy trench, with relatively precise accuracy.

World War I raised to a fine art the process of firing at targets that could not be seen by gun crews. Firing artillery at targets unseen by gun

development of IDF

crews is known as "indirect fire." To accomplish such a feat, an artillery unit needs observers who can spot targets and relay their coordinators on a map to a battery of artillery.

An American artillery battery of WWI usually consisted of four guns and was commanded by an officer who ranged in rank from a lieutenant to a major, but was most often a captain. Artillery observation ("spotting") is a most dangerous task since the observer must be in a vulnerable, and often exposed, position, like "no man's land," to spot enemy targets.

The artillery piece best suited for this type of objective is a Howitzer. Howitzers typically have short barrels that can be highly elevated, allowing them to fire large caliber projectiles to a great height so that they can fall rapidly at a sharp and precise angle, enabling an unseen enemy target to be obliterated.

The problem with the Howitzers of WWI was that they were very large and not easily moved by the horse teams or crude tractors and trucks of the era. This kept modest-sized field guns like the French 75 (which had a barrel capable of moderate elevation) relevant since they could be used to neutralize enemy targets, visible or not, and then moved relatively quickly by being attached to a caisson and limber and then drawn by a horse team to a new position on the battlefield. Terrain conditions, not size or weight, were the only real limitations to their rapid mobility.

With indirect fire, the observer provides the map coordinates, normally by field phone, of a "target of opportunity" to the battery's crew so they can adjust and aim their fire with a precise elevation of their gun's barrel in order to arch their shell and obtain a "direct hit" on their target. A so-called "target of opportunity" could be anything the scout could spot using his binoculars and then pinpointing on his map with his compass. This included anything from "masked" (hidden) enemy batteries, to enemy machine gun nests, or even high points such as hills or bell towers where any unseen enemy scout could be hiding.

All the while, the enemy's scouts were performing the very same function. A man like Len could instantly fall victim to a bullet fired by a well concealed enemy sniper, machine gun, or a single enemy shell fired precisely at his exact location, instantly atomizing him as soon as he heard the sound of the gun that fired such a shot. To survive, his actions would have

artillery organization & tactics

to be quicker, cleverer, and more precise than his enemy counterpart's and he would then have to move rapidly to a new, and hopefully less visible, position. His powers of observation and "feel" for the enemy would have to be sharp if he were to remain alive.

Each artillery battery had an officer who served as battery commander (BC). His job was to plot the position communicated from the scout on his corresponding map and then use trigonometry to calculate the range, trajectory, and fuse time while considering wind speed and deflection necessary to strike the designated target.

The scout in turn observed the incoming fire from the battery and phoned back any necessary adjustments necessary to make certain the shells were falling where intended. If the artillery fire fell on a target such as approaching enemy infantry or tanks, the scout would respond by saying something like, "Dead on!" or "On target!"

If the shells were falling, say, two hundred yards to the left of the target and a hundred yards short, the scout would respond on the field phone with something like, "two hundred right, add one hundred!" The scout gave the left/right (horizontal) corrections first, followed by the distance (vertical) correction. The process was repeated continuously until the scout was either killed by the enemy, or able to call in the final report of "target destroyed!"

Len might not be the one actually pulling the gun's lanyard that fired the fatal shots, but he was no less responsible for dealing out death since it was he who was effectively aiming the shellfire. It was all the more painful because he had to observe the results of artillery blowing men to bits, even correcting fire to catch enemy troops caught in the open and attempting in vain to retreat to safety before being atomized.

Len and the other scouts training with him learned about different types of artillery barrages. The "creeping" barrage (today, "rolling") is one that drops shells in a pattern, starting in no man's land and then advancing systematically toward the enemy's position. Friendly infantry uses the barrage from their artillery as cover to advance toward the enemy. This is especially dangerous, as the advancing infantry is at the complete mercy of the competence of their own scouts and BCs to prevent their deaths from "friendly fire" from their own guns.

Another barrage Len and his comrades learned about was for the defense of their own troops. A "box barrage" drops artillery shells on at least three, and often four sides, of their own men to protect them from advancing enemy infantry.

Len and the others also learned how to spot for a "Chinese Barrage" which is a barrage delivered with the intent of luring the enemy into artillery fire. Since artillery usually preceded infantry assaults in WWI, soldiers in the trenches immediately left their positions in the trenches at the start of a barrage for the safety of bunkers. After the barrage lifted, they quickly returned to their assigned positions to "stand to" and await the impending enemy assault.

The Chinese barrage was a strategy that employed a quick barrage followed by an equally quick lull. The enemy would return to their trench positions just in time to catch a second fresh barrage of shells and be blown to bits. It was in short, a deadly ruse.

The worst experience for Len was watching the poison gas splatter or seep from the first fired rounds of an artillery barrage that caught the Germans by surprise, without their gas masks. Even experienced men panicked as they clutched at their throats or cupped their hands over their now sightless eyes.

This was the expertise that Len obtained during his month at Valdahon. He and his comrades in the 58th FAB were now ready to be deployed to the front lines in the American sector near Verdun. Len's horse "Blackie" never made it to Europe—very few American horses did. He would need a new mount. Remount depot #4 at Valdahon had an ample selection of leftover crap.

The war had long since drained the British and French of their descent horses and almost everything left was nothing more than glue factory quality. Len chose the best he could from among the available selection, a mare named Annabel. She was 15-hands (60 inches) high and slender. Small and light, like many of the scouts themselves, these horses needed to carry their riders swiftly across the battlefield.

Cavalry boots were not waterproof and they were more subject to tearing, but they were considerably more comfortable that the "little tanks" worn by the infantry, and their agility made them far more practical for those riding horses. Len was also issued a canister model (British) gas mask, trench knife, and sidearm.

His training complete, and freshly equipped (including a new mount), Len and his comrades were ready to leave Valdahon and put their newly acquired skills for delivering death into practice. They might not want to do it but they would soon be blowing Huns to bits or dying while trying.

Observation platform: Artillery Scouts were sometimes alone as they moved to the furthest and highest points possible to observe the enemy and record his positions. Since field phones could be scarce, the scouts occasionally had to sketch what they observed and return quickly to their batteries with the target's coordinates.—Courtesy of Illinois National Guard

CHAPTER 5

· ·

Baptism By Fire

I T WAS AUGUST 23rd and Len was stunned by the reveille call, which
woke him from a sounder than usual sleep. It seemed somehow earlier
than normal and his head was still filled with cobwebs. The men were
groaning in unison as the electric lights overhead were being turned on and
the sergeants were yelling for everyone to fall out and gear up.

"It's only 2:00 am!" Someone blurted out as if it would somehow have
an effect on stopping this most unwelcomed jolt of reality. "Good Lord!"
Len thought to himself, "this is it! We're heading out to the battle lines!"
They were needed at the front and their superiors decided they had had
enough training. They were ready for a fight.

The men hustled and moved quickly to dress and grab their gear. They
were soon in ranks outside the barracks in the chilly night air as the moon
shown down brightly on them from above. An order was given for all those
assigned horses to get to the remount depot on the double and get their
mounts. The entire unit was moving out at 03:00. Len moved quickly to
Annabel's stall and took her reins to lead her out. Poor girl, she seemed as
dazed and surprised as he was. He couldn't help but wonder what fate
awaited them both.

Len was moving mechanically as he saddled Annabel and waited in
formation. A thought unnerved Len and made him quiver as he wondered
if he might not be advancing to his own death. While his conscious mind
wanted to resist his every movement, his body continued, without hesita-

tion, to proceed involuntarily forward as if controlled by unseen hands.

He glanced up at the Swiss Alps in the distance and thought of how a neutral world, free of armed conflict, was just over the other side. At that moment, he longed to be there and even envisioned himself crossing over as easily as crossing the street. But that was just a fleeting moment of fantasy. Len was accustomed to dealing with the here and now. He always accepted his responsibilities and the many hardships life had dealt him.

Len and everyone else waited anxiously as they were ordered to prepare to move out. It was quickly followed by a one-word directive, "MOUNT!" The men instantly climbed atop their horses in near perfect unison. They peeled from formation by sections and the stomping of army boots and horses' hooves, combined with the rolling wheels of caissons and supply wagons, filled the night air. Their movement was loud, but the men were silent. Obviously, Len thought to himself, he was not the only one pondering what fate awaited them on the battlefields ahead. As if his mind was not already gripped enough by concern, they temporarily shared the road with a civilian funeral procession. Len couldn't bring himself to look at it and averted his eyes until they were gone.

As they moved along, any civilians they passed were accustomed to seeing soldiers coming and going from Camp Le Valdahon. It had become a ritual occurring regularly over the last four years and had long since ceased to impress, or even much interest, the local bystanders.

The formation stopped to rest and eat in the afternoon. German observation planes occasionally flew overhead, but their mission was only to report American movements and not to attack them. The 58th FAB had been spotted to no effect, and the column got underway again. Anti-aircraft guns boomed in the distance as Boche planes appeared on and off again. Len was familiar with the road and despite the dimming light he could see their destination up ahead—Besançon. Len couldn't help but ponder the irony. The very place he had spent a few Sundays of leisure during his training would now serve as the staging area from which he and his comrades would be transported to the front. He couldn't help but feel a little betrayed by the town of which he had grown so fond. Today however, it was no longer the safe refuge from war concerns, as the beams from searchlights illuminated the night sky in search of enemy planes. Len now

felt sorry for beautiful Besançon as it, like the Doughboys, had been pre-
maturely robbed of its innocence by war.

The train at Besançon was segregated, as always, with the enlisted men
and horses in the "Cheaux-Huits" (forty-and-eights). The foul odor and
flea infestation were provided free of charge to every enlisted man's boxcar.
The caissons were loaded onto flat cars and covered with camouflage netting to conceal them from enemy view while the officers rode in (what
else?) rail carriages.

Stealth was now essential since the Germans had their mighty Gotha
Bombers flying nearby and, unlike observation planes, their bombers were
in the business of attacking. A train known to be carrying an artillery
brigade would be a most inviting target.

There were rest and water stops at Vesoul and Epinal. Everyone was
now ordered to be wearing their helmets ("tin hats") and to have their gas
masks readily available. There was more anti-aircraft fire at Epinal with no
result other than a great deal of noise. The train passed through Nancy
near the Toul sector, an American section of the front.

The ever-increasing number of American military personnel and visible
scars of war on the landscape, torn up rows of barbed wire and shell holes,
made it obvious they were nearing their destination. The train halted along
the Meuse River at a placed called Foug just north of Toul. The men and
horses were ordered out so that legs, human and equine, could be stretched
and the animals properly watered. As soon as the men and horses disembarked from the train, they were instantly drenched by a ferocious rainstorm that seemed to come out of nowhere. Len took Annabel and sought
shelter under an overhang connected to a patch of roof. No one had to be
reminded that their boots were not waterproof.

"Keep those horses dry," some lieutenant barked out as he passed up
and down the ranks. "Don't worry about us. We're fine too sir—you heartless bastard," Len thought to himself.

Half of the 58th Brigade would remain for the time being in Foug
while Len and the rest of the 124th would continue on to Pagny-sur-Meuse
and then Calvary. Calvary, Len thought, the same name as the place where
Christ was crucified. Len may have been a devout Catholic, something
that seemingly makes one immune to omens and superstitions, but all sol-

diers are superstitious, and he was no exception. Everyone knew that they were headed toward the St. Mihiel Sector and that sent a collective shiver down everyone's spine.

The St. Mihiel sector was a German salient taken from the French early in the war. A salient is a piece of land that protrudes like a finger into enemy territory. It borders the enemy's lines on three sides: it's top, bottom, and forward position. The St. Mihiel salient was high ground and contained the dreaded Mont Sec. It was a perfect observation point for German artillery spotters as they rained downed fire on their enemies, and the French had lost countless thousands in numerous, but futile, assaults to re-capture it. The job of taking it back was now going to fall to the fresh troops of the American Expeditionary Force.

The night was clear and crisp and the moon especially bright. The wheels of the caissons and artillery pieces were muffled with canvas rags, as were the horses' shoes. The order to mount was called out and Len and the others were instantly in their saddles. The orders were clear from this point on; no talking, no smoking, and a minimum distance of 25 yards was to be maintained at all times between the advancing artillery pieces. The fear of what might be in the darkness ahead kept Len's eyes sharp and wide.

In the wee hours of August 25th, Len and the 124th passed through Boucq where Y.M.C.A. personnel handed out two donuts per man as they passed along the road. The American Dogfaces of the next war might be said to be fighting for America, motherhood, and apple pie but the Doughboys of WWI thought of donuts long before apple pie. The treat was a welcome one. Along with the Y.M.C.A. and the Salvation Army, the American Red Cross did all they could to make this fattening staple available to provide the lonely Doughboys with a taste of home.

By 04:00 they reached the Forêt de la Reine. They entered the dense woods in a trance-like state to begin a wait of unknown duration for the orders that would soon send them forward to the front, now just a few miles ahead. The cannoneers dismounted, unhitched the horses, and everyone immediately dropped to the ground and went unconscious from near exhaustion.

The cannons and their caissons littered the roadway and could provide easy targets in the morning for German bombers or German artillery directed by the enemy's observation planes. Officers yelled orders for the men to wake up and move the pieces off the road. The only reply from the dense woods were the anonymous cries from Len and the others telling the officers what they could do to themselves. Since the officers had no immediate means of countering such insubordination, they were forced to move the equipment themselves. *whom —*

The next morning camouflage netting was raised to hide the guns, and official word was issued that horses were to be watered only at night. There were strict orders that no man, animal, or piece of equipment could be on the roads during daylight lest they be spotted by German planes. The area was ringed with some three-dozen French Hotchkiss machine guns as anti-aircraft protection. The guns, pointed upwards, were mounted on the wheels of uprighted axles. The axles, cut in two at their center, were in turn mounted in the back of trucks or wagons. This enabled operators to rotate the machine guns to fire at any enemy aircraft overhead. Len noticed how they chattered constantly and expended a great deal of ammunition, but never once saw an enemy plane hit.

In the meantime, there was nothing to do but enjoy the serenity of the woods and give thanks for every minute that ticked by, allowing them to remain behind the lines and relatively safe. While not yet at the actual front, they were still in a war zone. Along with anti-aircraft fire, Len observed aerial dogfights and French observation balloons ("sausages") that dotted the skyline; he also experienced occasional shelling from the Germans who targeted the woods every so often, just to let the Doughboys know their presence was highly suspected.

The horses were filled with piss and vinegar and Annabel was no exception. They wanted even less than the soldiers to be there and they hissed, snapped, and kicked at any human in their presence, but they could no longer intimidate their riders—fear of the Germans trumped anything the horses could mete out.

The following day, the rumor mill was in full swing as word spread among the ranks that the brigade was going up against the "impregnable" Mont Sec. Len was trying to convince himself that his loose stools were a result of diet, but feelings in the pit of his stomach signaled, in a way only a combatant can appreciate, that it was really the fear of approaching battle.

so the author can't appreciate it?

In the opening months of the war the Germans had made a quick drive to capture the strategically important city of Verdun and its fortifications. While they were halted by the French, the Germans had captured enough territory along the way to create a salient, named after the town, that was at its farthest point southwest and served as its apex—"St. Mihiel." The French referred to the salient in less flattering terms by simply dubbing it the "Hernia."

The salient was roughly 25 miles wide and 15 miles deep. This effectively cut off communication and traffic between the French cities of Verdun and Nancy, and provided a distinct advantage for the Germans—especially for their artillery that could now be directed with deadly accuracy from the high ground of Mont Sec to surrounding areas.

While St. Mihiel was the southern most pivot point of the salient, it was Mont Sec, now an impregnable German stronghold, that sat at the western tip of the salient. The French had made numerous attempts over the following years to retake Mont Sec and the salient. All of these attacks had been horrific failures and cost countless thousands of French soldiers their lives. Now it appeared this unenviable task would fall to Len and the other newly arrived Doughboys of the American First Army.

At first welcomed and refreshing, the boredom for the Doughboys in the woods soon became tedious. There were no drills, movements, or meaningful activities of any kind. Len even found himself joining in the popular pastime (and release of aggression) of destroying French coins by smashing the two-franc denominations into rings.

Len and the others could feel their tensions mount as trains filled with wounded passed them coming back from the front, while trucks filled with grave diggers passed in the opposite direction. It added a backdrop that kept everyone on edge and prone to the jitters.

Since August 26th, the 58th FAB had been assigned to provide fire support to the Eighty-Ninth and First Infantry Divisions. The "First" Division had been dubbed as such for being the first sizeable American infantry unit to arrive, and see significant action, in France. They were hard as nails, always in the thick of the action, and their presence was an omen that there would soon be serious fighting.

Some of the men of the First Division were moving up to the frontline

Len Fairfield at Camp Logan in Houston, Texas. Fairfield and the entire 33rd Infantry Division trained at Camp Logan from the start of November 1917 until May of 1918 when they departed for Camp Merritt in New Jersey and then Europe.

The French 75mm field gun, while somewhat overrated, was still one of the best artillery pieces of the war. It had a state of the art recoil system and could be fired very rapidly. It became the standard piece of the U.S. Army Field Artillery in France. The gun pictured here belonged to the American 6th Field Artillery Regiment, 1st Infantry Division and fired America's first (artillery) shot in anger on October 23, 1917.—*Courtesy of First Division Museum*

Rations were often thrown from army Liberty trucks to Doughboys returning from the front lines. Soldiers scooped up everything from chocolate and tobacco to tins of sardines and packs of hardtack.—*Courtesy of First Division Museum*

Standardized Christmas Cards, like this one from the American Red Cross, were issued to soldiers to mail to love ones back home. This card attempts to convey those convalescing from wounds as happy and content but few of the Doughboys had ever been far from home before and the separation, especially at Christmas, was hard on all of them.—*Courtesy of Illinois National Guard*

The static nature of World War I made artillery casemates something like the infantry dugouts in many trenches. Casemates housed large field guns along with; men, extensive amounts of ammunition (including gas shells), communications equipment, canned food, and an occasional memento of civilian comfort.—*Courtesy of First Division Museum*

American troops being trained on the use of a field phone. The signal corps worked closely with artillery scouts and even provided their training on field phones. The most common field phone used by the Americans was the M1914 service buzzer. It could receive and transmit via a headset or by a key to send Morse code. It was not wireless and enemy shells often severed cables disabling communication.
—*Courtesy of First Division Museum*

Camouflage netting and earth skillfully used to conceal an American gun battery. This type of elaborate cloaking was essential to avoid the prying eyes of enemy planes, balloons, and scouts who could call in counter battery fire and atomize the position.—*Courtesy of First Division Museum*

Artillery scouts had to venture to the furthest points forward to spot and relay targets of opportunity or the muzzle flashes from enemy guns. Notice the wires and field phone in the lower right. Scouting for the artillery was an exceptionally hazardous duty.—*Courtesy of First Division Museum*

Doughboys from the 33rd Infantry Division performing guard duty at a bridge in Wasserbillig, Luxembourg near the German border. The peacetime army could offer little beyond mundane duties to occupy the troops as they waited anxiously for the orders to return home.—*Courtesy of the Illinois National Guard*

Artillery Crews had to wait just like everyone else in the army. They waited for shells, food, water, and the order of when to move up in support of the infantry. The tedium is obvious on the face of one soldier looking directly into the camera.—*Courtesy of First Division Museum*

It was only during the final three months of the war, after breaking through
the static lines of the trenches, that the Allied armies became truly mobile.
Here, American supply wagons and gun crews move quickly to keep up with
the advancing infantry.—*Courtesy of First Division Museum*

Rolling Kitchens allowed Doughboys to enjoy hot grub in the field. The oven
on these flat wagons resembled an artillery piece resulting in their being dubbed
"Soup Cannons" by the troops.—*by permission from the World War I Museum*

Scouts and wagon crews water their horses on the outskirts of the shelled ruins at Cheppy during the Argonne Offensive.—*Courtesy of First Division Museum*

Artillery Scouts loading their horses aboard the famed French forty and eight (Quarante et Huit) boxcars so named for their ability to carry either 40 men or 8 horses. The horses needed to be rested and ready when they reached the front so, like their riders, they were taken to the front by rail.—*Courtesy of First Division Museum*

Above and below: The Salvation Army sent roughly 500 personnel to France. They often went where the rolling kitchens could not. They provided Doughboys with soup, sandwiches, hot coffee, lemonade, and donuts. Their willingness to go to the front lines and risk being gassed and shelled earned them the eternal gratitude and respect of America's fighting men.—*Courtesy of First Division Museum*

Salvation Army making Doughnuts under bardment of German Guns, Front Line-France.

A soldier from the signal corps taking down information inside a communications dugout. Headsets made oral communications possible but those using field phones and switchboards still had to be proficient in Morse code and trench ciphers used to code messages.—*Courtesy of First Division Museum*

The American troops in Luxembourg (like those pictured here) were designated as the Army of Occupation in Reserve. This distinction, unlike the Americans stationed in Germany and Austria-Hungary, made them ineligible for the occupation medal. Frequently assembled for announcements and proclamations, they waited in eager anticipation for the order to return home.—*Courtesy of First Division Museum*

Artillery pieces used in the First World War were most often hauled by horses or mules and always placed by men. The French 75 weighed just under a half ton and took several men to put into place. Battery commanders, artillery scouts, and any other military personnel nearby were often impressed into such service.—*Courtesy of First Division Museum*

Artillerymen watering their horses in a portable trough just behind the front lines. Horses were used on both sides by the cavalry, for the hauling of wagons and artillery pieces, as well as by artillery scouts. Horses quickly became a rare and highly valuable commodity. Soldiers assigned horses, or mules, were directly responsible for their care and it was not a matter to be taken lightly.—*Courtesy of First Division Museum*

Soldiers of any era are often too preoccupied, or simply unable to find paper, to write home. During the Great War, the U.S. military wanted to do all it could to keep the home fires burning so soldiers, marines, and sailors were required to date, sign, address, and fill in the blanks of standardized cards announcing their safe arrival in Europe or return back to the states.—*Courtesy of Illinois National Guard*

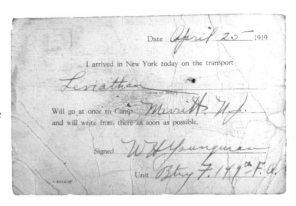

By the autumn of 1918 it was obvious, even to German soldiers, that the Allies would soon be victorious and prisoners were taken in ever growing numbers. Here, smiling German POWs are all too happy to be alive in captivity with their role in the war over.—*Courtesy of Illinois National Guard*

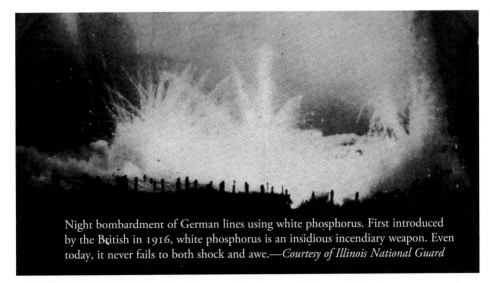

Night bombardment of German lines using white phosphorus. First introduced by the British in 1916, white phosphorus is an insidious incendiary weapon. Even today, it never fails to both shock and awe.—*Courtesy of Illinois National Guard*

The American and French assault on St Mihiel brought some 3,000 artillery pieces to bear on the defending Germans. It was the biggest artillery barrage on the Western Front since the Battle of Verdun which lasted throughout almost all of 1916. Here, Doughboys are working on a hillside directing a row of field guns towards Mont Sec on the St Mihiel Salient just prior to the battle.—*Courtesy of First Division Museum*

Doughboys scatter as German shells whistle in on their position. Americans referred to enemy shells as "iron cigars" and "GI (galvanized iron) cans." The body of a dead German soldier is lying in the street alongside an FT-17 Renault light tank. The United States requisitioned just over 500 French Renaults for use by the AEF.—*Courtesy of First Division Museum*

Above and below: Scouts were trained, and usually operated, as a team of two men to observe enemy movements and targets. They verified each others observations and one man was responsible for using the field phone if one was available. The soldier in the foreground is sketching and/or writing down target co-ordinates.—*Both photos courtesy the First Division Museum.*

Makeshift American Cemetery near Mountfaucon. Some 26,000 Doughboys were killed in the Argonne Offensive. The highest number of American dead of any US battle ever.—*Courtesy of Illinois National Guard*

Some French towns simply ceased to exist as a result of the incessant artillery barrages. Here is a typical main street of a French village in Lorraine after American shelling forced the Germans out. Engineers cleared rubble from the streets quickly in order to allow supply trains and artillery batteries to keep up with advancing infantry.—*Courtesy of Illinois National Guard*

These Doughboys are in a forward trench wearing French M-2 gas masks. The M-2s were nowhere near as effective as the British small box respirators and, by the autumn of 1918, use of the M-2 was banned altogether by American commanders.—*Courtesy of Illinois National Guard*

Live steam was brought to the front on American Liberty trucks or British Foden Lorries to delouse the uniforms of soldiers. Here, obviously amused Americans strip down for the process. Soldiers often bathed in the open out of pans of soapy water as they waited for their uniforms. The process was largely futile for artillerymen as they were instantly re-infested once they came into contact with the hay that was used for their bedding and to feed their horses.
—*Courtesy of First Division Museum*

The French 75mm gun could fire both high explosive (HE) and shrapnel shells at a rate of 15 rounds per minute. The mountain of shell casings here attests to the gun's rapid rate of fire. *Courtesy of First Division Museum*

Doughboys posing by a Model M1914 Hotchkiss machine gun. The AEF requisitioned some 7,000 of these guns from the French. The cartridges were feed into the weapon on a horizontal strip that held 24 rounds of 8mm ammunition. This particular gun is mounted on the wheel of an up righted axle for use as an anti-craft ("Archie") weapon. *Courtesy of First Division Museum*

trenches near the salient, when Len and the other "cannon fodder" (those not yet tried by combat and thus considered highly expendable) were treated to an impromptu lecture. It was complete with details of how bloated corpses were bayoneted in the abdomen by the graves registration unit in order to release pent up gases that caused bloating and swelling among the dead that littered the battlefield. *low diction*

The lecture also included the "fact" that mustard gas, which works on any moist parts of the body, required castration among the victims unfortunate enough to have sweaty balls at the time of an attack (as if a soldier could avoid sweaty balls, or sweaty anything, at the time of an attack). Naturally, some rube had to ask if that included urine covered balls from pissed pants. "Oh, that's even worse," was the reply. "In that case, a feller's entire cock gets wet and would probably have to come off." What a cheery thought, Len mused. *Where do these quotes come f/?*

Almost all the Doughboys wrote puns on their gas masks. Having worked for the gas works before the war, Len scrawled, "People's Gas, Light & Coke Co.," on his. "I'll probably die in the first gas attack," Len thought to himself. "I won't be able to breath the air with the mask off and I can't breath at all with the damn thing on."

The Americans referred to incoming German artillery as "iron cigars" or "G.I. (galvanized iron) cans." The Germans were lobbing occasional shells from their siege guns at their newly arrived enemy, but almost all without success. The sole exception was a direct hit on an abandoned barn being used as a makeshift ammo facility. It caused quite a raucous but amazingly produced no casualties.

The Americans were quick to return the favor. Batteries A and B had some 90mm guns southeast of Rambucourt at the northern end of Forêt de la Reine, and on September 3rd began to return fire to register their guns and generally harass the enemy. It would continue somewhat sporadically right up until the beginning of the battle, but without the active participation of the scouts.

An entrepreneurial Frenchman benefited from the fortunes of war by turning his former house into a café. It was crude but popular and provided a nice diversion from the day's monotony. After almost 10 days in the woods and only sporadically firing their guns, the Doughboys were beginning to wonder aloud how much longer their reprieve could last. First Division Infantry troops and their guns, along with other artillery units, continued to pass by them on their way to the front. Something really big was in the works and Len and his compatriots continued with dread to await the order for their unit to move up with the others.

Finally, their luck ran out. Almost as soon as the American guns began firing, the orders came to "move up!" Though American engineers had paved the road leading out of the forest and to the trenches, it was a complete cluster fuck of military vehicles, equipment, and personnel of every kind milling about. Military police were trying to direct traffic and enforce the standard distance of 50 meters between vehicles, without much success. Len couldn't help but feel his stomach sink as their unwieldy caravan neared the frontlines.

As they neared Broussey-Raulecourt, Len was amazed that so much of the village was still intact. The church steeple had been taken out by German artillery, but that was standard operating procedure—every soldier knew that elevated points were always used by snipers or artillery scouts to plot fire. The foreboding and dreaded Mont Sec was just ahead in the foreground. Len knew without a doubt that this was to be their objective.

They continued another two miles forward into Bouconville. The town had been shelled almost entirely into rubble. The use of artillery and machine guns in this area had been so intense that as many as one thousand men a minute had been killed in action during the ferocious battles for Mont Sec. In the Bouconville area, Batteries A and B would be placed at Le Joli Bois. Battery C would be situated in Rambucourt. The Brigade's Post Command (P.C.) was in Boucq.

Len and the other observers knew they would have to move forward from Bouconville (northwest of Verdun) and from Rambucourt (southeast of Verdun) when the time for battle arrived. The entire idea behind their unit's formation was to have rapidly moving field artillery that could keep up with the infantry's driving advances, while continuing to provide them with fire support.

If they did their jobs well, they could direct artillery fire capable of blasting fortifications and thousands of Germans into atoms. If they failed, they could watch as thousands of advancing French and American troops were cut down by enemy machine guns and artillery. Either way, their hands would be dripping with blood.

From high ground around Bouconville, Len and the others were observing the amazing sight of an intact church steeple in Rambucourt that would do well for observation. They momentarily envied Battery C's good fortune. The Germans, however, realized this same fact and soon their shells began to pepper the town and destroyed the steeple, while frustrated Doughboys could only take cover and watch in helpless exasperation.

It was now that the real work began at Le Joli Bois for Len and every other Doughboy in the 124th. Casemates, a form of artillery foxhole, had to be dug to place cannons (French 75mms) and their crews in. One casemate contained a battery (four cannons and their crews) that was then covered with burlap netting overhead, supported by a group of four poles to form a camouflage canopy. Guns and crews were placed inside the casemate and then covered with the canopy. This was all well and good except that earlier movement of infantry in the same area had so trampled the surrounding ground that the freshly camouflaged casemates stood out, rather than blend in.

The Germans zeroed their artillery in on one of these inviting targets and instantly killed two men, providing the 58th Field Artillery Brigade with their first combat deaths. Enemy shellfire also took out an ammo dump.

Everyone was in nervous silence the next day as more casemates were completed, equipment checked, and scouting parties returned from patrols. When Len and the others returned to the Forêt de la Reine, they were exhausted. The standard frontline staples of beans, Willy, slum, and hot java were waiting. They would need to continue waiting.

Orders came in for the batteries to prepare to receive a shipment of 2,000 high explosive (H.E.) shells. This meant that once again Len and every other man would have to return to Bouconville to assist in placing the rounds in ammo dumps and casemates. There would be no time for supper. The trucks were due to start arriving at 21:00 hours (9:00 p.m.). Len couldn't help but wonder how the German gunners would be salivating when they heard all this noise, knowing that men would be exposed everywhere.

The trucks were four hours late and unable to traverse the muddy slopes up to the trench lines, so their cargo had to be unloaded roughly a quarter mile short of their intended destination. This turned out to be something of a mixed blessing since it meant Germans couldn't hear the noisy vehicles approaching.

On the down side, a box of artillery ammo consisted of nine shells with each shell weighing fifteen pounds. It took two men considerable effort to carry a one hundred and thirty five pound box the necessary distances. Some fourteen trucks, each carrying sixteen boxes, hauled what turned out to be 234 boxes (2106 shells), or more than 31,000 pounds, of high explosives to men who had to then schlep them manually almost a quarter mile uphill in muddy terrain! The job was completed in two hours, causing Len and every other Doughboy to be racked with pain and fatigue.

Len was able, with effort, to pull himself atop Annabel, and was getting ready for the ride back to the safety of Broussey-Raulecourt where he could collapse, when a second supply train of ammo trucks arrived with an additional one thousand artillery shells. Despite an argument between the officers and the truck drivers, there was no way to return, and nowhere to place the unwanted shells, so they were simply dumped along the roadside in ditches. The problem now was that the sun would be coming up in less than two hours and there would be no time to remove them from the view of German observation planes. Camouflage netting was thrown over the crates and Len and the others continued into Raulecourt.

Len was asleep for only an hour when he was awakened by banging klaxons and pans resounding everywhere. "GAS! It's a gas attack!" was the shriek heard from nearly every pup tent and billow. Len scrambled for his mask and then dashed out to put Annabel's on in the allotted time. Annabel, possibly claustrophobic, had long since realized this contraption was not a feedbag and provided considerable resistance. It took Len something like fifteen minutes to get the damned thing on her. Everywhere there was confusion and panic as Doughboys scrambled to find their masks. Fortunately, it was all for naught—a false alarm. "Probably some idiot farting up silent gas bombs in his pup tent," Len thought to himself.

On September 5th Len and his compatriots were back in Bouconville.

Everything was being made ready for battle and every Doughboy knew that their first great assault was not far off. Casemates were still being dug everywhere. During a break, as Len sat on some ammo boxes with a few others and had begun to sip hot coffee, they noticed a strange odor and an irritation in their eyes. A moment later klaxons sounded and screams of "GAS!" echoed everywhere.

Again, the panicked ritual of scrambling for and putting on gas masks, as well as doing the same for the horses, went into practice. It was several minutes before someone figured out that they were not under attack. The odor and eye irritation was their reaction to the fresh paint and turpentine from the newly erected camouflage netting! "Our 'canaries' (gas officers) don't seem to be worth a damn," Len mused.

The next day, Len's Company A was nicely situated with a field mess converted from an old barn. A nearby lake provided fresh water for coffee and shaving and everything seemed just Jake. Then, a problem arose when one of the boats bringing shells across the lake to a forward casemate over-turned. Some Doughboys immediately stripped down and dove in after them. They surfaced with the shells and bleached white faces as they dis-covered to their horror that the entire lake bottom was covered with thou-sands of skeletons of dead French soldiers from the slaughter that had been Mont Sec.

There was no shortage of vomiting men, and the Doughboys couldn't dump their coffee fast enough. They immediately dubbed the body of water "Skeleton Lake" and returned to the use of water from nearby wells for drinking and shaving.

On September 7th, Len and his compatriots were busy digging still more casemates when they were forced to take shelter as German shells began landing in their sector. Len was well schooled and soon realized that the Heinies (a derogatory term for the German enemy taken from the name Heinrich) were only adjusting their guns to register their range. The shells were intentionally being directed from a German plane onto an area that was free of American personnel. This was an example of the famed, "live and let live" philosophy that the combatants of the Great War often embraced to provide themselves a brief reprieve from the incessant slaughter of the trenches. Still, Len did not much appreciate the kindness in the situation, as the rocking ground and flying debris caused a stirring in his bowels that he hoped he wouldn't end up carrying in the seat of his pants.

With the shelling over, final casemates were dug that night and the guns put into place with great silence. The Eighteenth Regiment (1st Infantry Division) passed through their ranks on their way to the front trenches. Everyone, on both sides, knew the big push was rapidly approaching. Nerves were tense and Len was no exception. He found comfort in praying the rosary he carried in his pants pocket and he incessantly checked Annabel's shoes and hooves for any possible flaw. His equipment was ready and he waited, almost with eagerness, for the order to move up to a forward position for observation. He felt the order to finally do something would be a relief after the eternal waiting and worrying.

While the Americans were preparing for a massive offensive, they were unaware that the Germans now believed that Mont Sec, and the rest of the St. Mihiel Salient, could no longer be held and were making preparations to abandon the salient and move eastward to consolidate their lines.

The Germans had been siphoning off their better troops from the St. Mihiel Salient since 1916 and by the summer of 1918, the Germans' commanding General of the area, Max von Gallwitz, was anticipating an American attack. He had a mere 23,000 troops with which to defend his position. The Americans, on the other hand, would be attacking with ten times that number with an additional 110,000 French troops in support!

Gallwitz had devised a plan ("Loki") that would allow for a twelve-day evacuation period from the salient. The first eight days would be devoted to removing weapons and equipment and the remaining four to personnel. Gallwitz's delay in acting on his plan would result in the worst possible scenario for his forces. They would end up withdrawing, in the open and at their most vulnerable, just as the Americans would begin their massive offensive.

That was still a few days away in the future. At the immediate moment, Len could feel his arms throb as he swung a pick, ripping out the timber shorings of the casemate which had originally been dug by the French early in the war to house two of their De Bange 90mm cannons. By this time in the war, the De Bange was an obsolete artillery piece. This particular casemate had to be widened to hold the four French 75mms of the 124th's Battery A. When the shorings were out, Len and the others put down their picks and exchanged them for shovels so they could begin the arduous task of widening the damned hole.

Battery A was commanded by First Lieutenant John W. McCarthy, who kept a watchful eye on the casemate's preparations as well as the care of his guns and their crews. Once the casemate was widened, things were still far from over. Len picked up a sledge hammer with his bruised and blistered hands so that spikes could be driven into the wooden planking that the engineers had dropped off to shore up the earthworks that were to serve as Battery A's new casemate and home. Len contemplated the passion of Christ as he drove himself seemingly beyond all bodily endurance and wondered how his suffering, much lest the Passion, was possible.

The preparation of the casemate had taken the entire day and gone into the evening. It was not until after midnight that the guns and shells arrived for placement. Len and the others were drenched in sweat and near collapse. Nature then seemed to mock them as it began to rain and the temperature dropped.

The telephone dugout, also home of the artillery scouts, was established to the rear of the artillery pieces so at least there would be a place to be dry and relatively comfortable. It wasn't the Ritz, but a hell of a lot better than the casemates and trenches. At that moment, Len longed for the order to go to the telephone dugout more than one to go home to Chicago. He was dog-tired and the dugout was a lot closer than home.

All the hauling and placement of guns and shell boxes had to be done in the mud and dark. This was the type of misery and drudgery that Len and the other Doughboys so detested. "General Sherman was right," Len said to Al. "War is hell!" Al grinned and expounded, "Obviously, he wasn't just referring to the fighting."

Each artillery piece had to be brought forward, mounted on a caisson pulled by a team of six horses. Each casemate housed four guns. One gun was designated as the "base piece" (the one which fired the initial shot; the not other three were used to adjust their fire), and that was placed first. All exa four of the guns were aimed at Mont Sec. Len and his comrades then staggered back to the telephone dugout for breakfast and some much needed rest. Len had just been up for 24 hours straight and been doing hard physical labor during most of it. Upon arriving, he fell asleep without any thought of food or drink.

Len and the others were awakened after only six hours to return to their battery's casemate. The shells they had unloaded would now have to be separated according to their designated use. There were fragmentation shells for raining shrapnel down on the enemy, as well as high explosive shells (H.E.) for reducing enemy fortifications, layers of barbed wire, and any other strong points. There were also chemical shells filled with gas (gaz) #5, Hydrocyanic (Hydrogen Cyanide) as well as "White Cross" or "White Star," a combination of chlorine and phosgene designed to destroy the lungs. Shells had to be ever-so-carefully removed from their cases and placed in the appropriate billet selected for the corresponding type of shell.

Though Len didn't know it then, the offensive had originally been set to begin about this time, but the inexperience of the Americans' logistical support had delayed everything. The problem was that this was obvious to everyone including the enemy. The fortunate aspect, and great blessing to the American forces, was that the Germans were not using this time to re-enforce their positions but rather to begin withdrawing. Von Gallwitz was acting almost as slowly as the Americans, but he was moving.

By the 10th of September, the French and American infantry were in place. The Field Artillery was ready to go. The tension was so tight it could be cut with a knife. Humor served to disarm the situation as the rolling kitchens, first American and then French, came up to the front with all the noise of a Midwestern April tornado. Len and the others stood in awed silence as this comical parade swept past their unit at breakneck speed and continued up the road.

Len and the other Doughboys had gone to considerable lengths to camouflage their casemates but the French were setting up artillery positions in the open without even a casemate! They fired on the Germans for a while and then sat down in the open to have their supper.

Len and the others were kept occupied with busy work. There was the checking and re-checking of equipment, animals, and one's nerve. Battery A was regarded by command as the best disciplined in the Brigade, and even Len's worries had given way to a desire to be done with the whole damn thing. The sooner the fight, the sooner they could end the damn war and go home.

The next day had more rain, cool temperatures and fog, but that was not such a bad thing. The fog kept the prying eyes of German planes and ground observers from having anything meaningful to report. The word had gone through the ranks that the fight would start before sunup the next day. The Battle of St. Mihiel was where the U.S. military originated the terms "D-Day" and "H-Hour."

Len and the other Doughboys were issued yellow tubes of Anti-Gas Ointment #2 for topical use for those whose skin suffered exposure to mustard gas. Everyone could hear in the rear the sound of FT-17 Renault tanks clamoring up the road at the robust speed of four-miles-per-hour. They were under the command of some wild-eyed, swashbuckling cavalryman by the name of George Patton.

D-Day was set for September 12th with H-Hour at 0500. The 58th FAB was assigned to the American IV Corps. The IV Corps was made up of the 89th ("Rolling W"), 42nd ("Rainbow"), and 1st ("Big Red One") Infantry Divisions. The 58th would be positioned at the far left western end of the IV Corps in the Apremont Forest (Apremont-la-Forêt). Their position would abut the French II Colonial Corps.

The primary objective of the 58th FAB was to provide fire support for the 1st Division as they went "over the top." The entire American First Army, newly formed and eager as hell, was about to go headlong into the fray, and as a scout for the artillery unit assigned to the 1st Division, Len would be in one of the thickest parts of the fight.

Chapter overall –

moving up to front –

First encounter w/ enemy fire.

Calm before the storm.

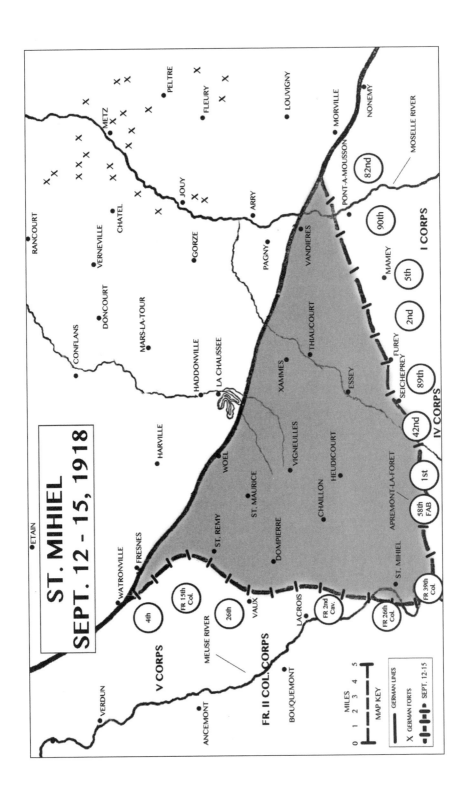

ST. MIHIEL
SEPT. 12 - 15, 1918

MILES
0 1 2 3 4 5

MAP KEY

✗ GERMAN FORTS

▬▬ GERMAN LINES

▬▪▬▪▬ SEPT. 12-15

I CORPS

82nd
90th
5th
2nd
89th

IV CORPS

42nd
1st
58th FAB
FR 39th Col.

FR. II COL. CORPS

FR 26th Col.
FR 2nd Cav.
26th
FR 15th Col.

V CORPS

4th

MOSELLE RIVER
MEUSE RIVER

PELTRE
FLEURY
LOUVIGNY
MORVILLE
NONEMY
PONT-A-MOUSSON
METZ
JOUY
ARRY
CHATEL
VERNEVILLE
GORZE
PAGNY
VANDIERES
MAMEY
RANCOURT
DONCOURT
MARS-LA-TOUR
CONFLANS
THIAUCOURT
FUREY
SEICHEPREY
ESSEY
HADDONVILLE
LA CHAUSSEE
XAMMES
HARVILLE
WOEL
VIGNEULLES
HEUDICOURT
CHAILLON
APREMONT-LA-FORET
ST. MAURICE
DOMPIERRE
ST. REMY
WATRONVILLE
FRESNES
VAUX
LACROIX
ST. MIHIEL
ETAIN
VERDUN
ANCEMONT
BOUQUEMONT

CHAPTER 6

. . . .

St. Mihiel: The Americans
Enter the War in Earnest

RENCH GENERAL FERDINAND Foch, the Supreme Commander
of Allied forces in France, had proposed in July of 1918 a strategy
to drive the Germans out of France, back to the Hindenburg Line
along their own border, and into capitulation before year's end. The addition of American personnel and money now gave him almost limitless resources to conduct war against a foe rapidly fading out of existence. Under
Foch's plan, the Germans would become the anvil forced to absorb relent-
less blows from the Allied hammer.

Foch believed that the destruction of the German salients at Amiens
(Australian, Canadian, British, French—and a small American—sector),
the Marne (French & American sector), and St. Mihiel (also French and
American sector) would form a solid and easily maneuverable Allied line
from which he could then deliver the death blow to what remained of the
German Army and win the war for the Allies. The plan has been recorded
in history as the "100 Days Campaign," as well as "The Grand Offensive."

The strategy obviously was working. The Allied counter-offensive
began at the Second Battle of the Marne (Soissons to the Americans) in
mid-July and then progressed to the north at Amiens on August 8th.
Amiens met with quick success, as 16,000 enemy troops surrendered almost immediately in what German Commander Erich Ludendorff referred
to as "the Black Day of the German Army."

Len and everyone else knew on September 11th that they were on the eve of another "big push." It could be felt as much as the cold and rain that permeated everything. The men were ordered to check their personal equipment as the gun crews made their final preparations.

Len and the others were given their gas masks. They were not issued the British canister style to which they were accustomed, but rather the French Tissot models. The French masks had the innovative design of air valves under the eyepieces so that the lens would not fog over. Gloves ("oilcloth mitts") were dispensed as well. It was very frightening; every man knew this was for protection from mustard gas ("yellow cross") that the Germans now used with great frequency.

Len and his companions had been exposed to tear gas in training, but mustard gas was unknown amongst their experiences and the unknown is always the most frightening. The personal weapons, for Len a trench knife and .45 caliber colt sidearm, were checked. He wouldn't be taking a rifle or Annabel for this action. For one, poor Annabel would sink in the water-filled mud holes and drown. The mud swallowed men and animals faster than quicksand, and for another, he'd be repositioned in a dugout before the fight began.

Germans wearing American uniforms in order to cause additional chaos and confusion on the battlefield was not a tactic that originated with the Ardennes (Bulge) Offensive of World War II. English speaking Germans had been reported wearing the uniforms of captured American officers and, during the high point of battle, running up and down U.S. lines ordering a hasty retreat. A clever and deceptive tactic if ever there was one! Len and the others had been ordered not to heed any such directives unless it was from officers they recognized—the obvious caveat being that their own officers did not become casualties. Unknown officers seen issuing such orders were to be shot on sight.

The thought of approaching battle raced through Len's mind. This would no longer be practice or drill but the real thing. "It might all end for me tomorrow," he thought to himself. Nothing to do now but put it all in God's hands. How could he worry after an inspiration came to mind, from his Douay-Rheims Bible, Matthew 6:27, "and which of you by taking thought, can add to his stature by one cubit?" In other words buddy, worry can't do a thing to add one second to your life.

Still, despite near exhaustion, he wouldn't even attempt sleep. Just as well. Noise from the incessant rain was hardly conducive for sleep, and word was already out among the artillery's ranks that the fireworks would start with a barrage at 01:00 hours, lasting until the infantry went in at 05:00.

A lieutenant came into the communications dugout to brief the scouts and told them that they'd be doing just one thing—observing. There would be no alterations or corrections in the angle of fire once the battle began except to neutralize any enemy guns that were spotted returning fire. "The tunnels of Mont Sec have already been pre-sighted," the lieutenant said. "Every field piece will fire three shots a minute of Number-five gas until daylight. If you did your calculations correctly, and the batteries sighted properly, there won't be a Heinie left alive in those holes when our boys get there."

Despite Mont Sec being the prying eyes and ears of the Germans' artillery, Len couldn't help but feel some small degree of sympathy for the enemy in the tunnels of Mont Sec. Gas No. 5 was Hydrocyanic (Hydrogen Cyanide) gas. It usually killed in less than a minute. The enemy would most likely be inhaling a fatal dose before they even knew they were being gassed and thus have no time for putting on their masks.

Len and Al Slowey were ordered to take a position in a dugout near a forward ridge where the signal corps would have a service buzzer waiting for them. They would be within American lines and flanked by their own infantry for protection. Field glasses, trench knife with sidearm, along with water and rations were all that were necessary for them to bring. This was intended to be the beginning of their on-the-job training as artillery scouts.

Their orders and mission clear, Al and Len fell in with some signal corps and infantry and began to slosh their way to their assigned post. The mud was thick and the men walked on anything that aided in keeping them out of it. "Duckboards," boards nailed together in the form of elongated pallets, were sometimes present but normally reserved for use in the bottom of the infantry's deep trenches. Len had heard stories of soldiers who had supposedly fallen into watery shell holes with muddy bottoms so gripping that, even holding ropes thrown to them, they could not be pulled out by their comrades. The men would beg to be shot as they sank into the bottom of a muddy abyss.

A gallows humor for men on horseback was that the rider stood a better chance of survival so long as his waist remained above water and he could get his feet out of the stirrups. That made it possible for someone to pull him to safety. These thoughts gave Len a shudder; even when masked by humor there was no denying that the muddy earth did in fact consume living men.

When they reached their observation post, Al and Len slithered into the dugout through its rear. Sopping wet, cold, and muddy they prepared to check the service buzzer and ready their field glasses. Al put on the headphones and checked them. His audio transmission was acknowledged. He then used the Morse lever to send a single letter, "R" which was "acknowledgement." The communications dugout in the rear responded immediately with the letter "P" which was "affirmative." They were ready. Len peered through his binoculars in the distance at Mont Sec. It would all begin very soon.

At 1:00 a.m. sharp, a ground-based naval gun fired a shot that fell near Hill 390. Then a chorus of artillery immediately followed. The volleys continued without interruption as the ground quaked and the horizon was awash in flashes. There were so many artillery pieces firing that it was impossible to distinguish individual shots and it often sounded like one continuous roar. Len's ears were ringing without relief.

It seemed there wasn't a square inch of enemy-held ground that was being spared from American shells. Len handed his binoculars to Al who looked out on the barrage. The two men then looked at each other, their eyes wide and their mouths open in awe. No need, or even use, saying anything, as their thoughts were the same and neither man would be able to hear the other anyway.

Len wondered if there might not be any salient left for the infantry to attack once the four-hour-long bombardment came to a close. He was also watching closely for muzzle flashes from enemy guns. German artillery, if spotted, would have to be located by the scouts and reported so the American guns could provide counter-battery fire and quickly neutralize it, but Len and Al could see nothing coming from the enemy's lines. If there were any Germans alive and capable of returning fire, it was undetectable and obviously ineffective.

What Len and the rest of the American forces did not yet know was that the barrage had caught the Germans at their worst possible moment— just as they were withdrawing. The German 10th and 77th Reserve Divisions were in the process of pulling out at the start of the battle and were caught out in the open, obviously the most fatal place to be during an artillery barrage. Many of the Germans' 77th Divisional guns were destroyed in place before they could even return fire. This was the most intense artillery barrage on the Western Front in two years. Not since the yearlong battle of Verdun in 1916 had anyone seen anything like this.

As 5:00 a.m. approached, the rain slowed to a light drizzle and then stopped altogether. Flares of various colors were being shot into the air by Very (flare) pistols as artillery fire slowed dramatically. Whistles then sounded and the First Division Infantrymen went over the top toward the southwest portion of the salient. At the same time, the French II Colonial Corps began their advance from the west. Other American units simultaneously began moving up all along the southern section of the salient.

The artillery flared back up again with a creeping barrage in support of the infantry and the sound of machine guns added to the chorus of death. It continued unabated until 11:00 a.m. when Al picked up Morse code on the service buzzer relaying the letters, "C F" (cease firing) to all units. It was quiet on Mont Sec now and the piece of real estate that had been so important to the Allied effort in the Verdun Sector, the same area that had cost the French countless thousands of men, was now back in Allied hands.

The rain started up again as kitchen personnel brought up soup, sandwiches and hot coffee. Len and the others with him in the dugout had little interest. Few Doughboys had slept the night before and anyone who could was simply going to sleep wherever they were, even if it meant just laying down in the mud to do it.

The stomping of marching feet and the rattle of equipment clanking together startled Len and Al back into consciousness. The wounded were returning and with them German POWs under the escort of First Division men. The two men looked out from their dugout at the rabble that was passing by them. "There's no doubt this war is nearing the end," Len said. "Look at that, will you just look at that?" Len said to Al. "They're just boys!

Boys in uniforms! They should be in school." It seemed the great Army of Prussia, the dreaded Hun who threatened to conquer the world and eradicate democracy were down to drafting boys in their mid-teens. There were some grizzled old veterans as well, but most every POW seemed happy enough to have their part in the war over and be in the blessed safety of captivity.

American and French supply trains were moving up rapidly and in huge numbers. The roads soon clogged with traffic, but Len and Al were too tired to care or to be kept from sleep any longer. Their respite was to be short lived. The order to move forward came around suppertime when it was obvious that the Germans would not be conducting a counter attack. Mont Sec, now seemingly devoid of even a blade of grass, was simply a matter for after-action reports and the history books. The infantry was moving forward at breakneck speed toward new objectives and the 58th FAB, a circus unit, had been designed and trained to keep pace with it. The guns were limbered and the men and caissons rolled out toward the Commune (township) of Xivray near Nonsard at 20:00 hours.

As Len and Al exited the dugout and approached the road, they were thrown some cans of willy and some hard bread from a passing supply wagon. "I wonder what they're eating back home," Al muttered. "I'd settle for some of that hot coffee we missed earlier," Len responded.

It was typical of the army's standing operating procedure of hurry up and wait. First, while Len and Al were sleeping, the artillery pieces had been limbered and then unlimbered for fear of enemy counter fire. Enemy fire never materialized so now, with the guns limbered once again, it was time to move up.

The scouts' horses were still well to the rear, so the two men fell in with the rest of the eclectic mob forming on the road; there were French ration wagons, American infantry, French machine gunners, American caissons, aerial (balloon) observers, and military police who tried in vain to keep things moving in good order. Everything advanced at a snail's pace if it moved at all. The column wound through Bouconville, passed Skeleton Lake, and then into Rambucourt where the road finally started to open up. Len was amazed at the absolute havoc that their artillery had brought about. Mont Sec was glowing in the distance. It was obvious that the village was ablaze. The intermittent explosions in the distance were not cannon fire but the Germans destroying their own ammo dumps as they retreated.

Len and the rest of the 124th were ordered to peel off from the long column while the 123rd went in the opposite direction. The battery would take up position along a line of scrub just off the road. The guns were put in place and just before 4:00 a.m. on September 13th, Len and his compatriots were given the OK to crawl into the wet brush and get some sack time.

In the morning, as Len and the others pulled themselves from their slumber, the sun revealed the ruins of war. Shattered homes around them and ahead of them, nothing but mud and shell holes of what had been up until yesterday the no man's land between the German and Allied lines.

There were numerous Renault FT-17s, French tanks supplied for Patton's very first armored push. Covered with camouflage paint, American markings, and a playing card from a poker deck painted on each, the "mechanized horses" had rotating turrets and were operated by two-man crews. They were intended to perform the work of ancient cavalry on modern battlefields. Unfortunately, Patton's tanks failed to live up to expectations. They were now out of action, mostly from simply falling into trenches and shell holes from which they couldn't extricate themselves. Their empty steel shells now littered the smoldering battlefield.

The 1st Infantry Division, the unit whom the 58th FAB was to be supporting, was nowhere to be found. They had continued their advance and were far ahead of their supporting artillery.

The signal corps had phone lines up, connecting the 58th with the front which was now well to the north, so the officers gave the orders to limber the guns and advance into the town of Nonsard. Len put some hard bread into his mouth and took a swig of coffee. They were far enough to the rear to allow for cooking fires and this time he did not miss out on the hot coffee being dispensed.

The stable crews had not yet caught up with the guns, so Annabel was still on her way forward. Len's dogs (feet) were barking, and he murmured unpleasantries under his breath as he fell into formation with other similar unfortunates. With everyone in formation and carriages and cais-

sons ready, the order "Forward, Yoh!" echoed down the line and the column began to roll.

Reconnaissance parties had been up to Mont Sec and were reporting
back. Word spread quickly amongst the ranks. It was a sight to behold.
The Heinies had real brass balls. They had converted the town into the
closest thing resembling a resort that military circumstances could allow.
They had some really cozy quarters.

Then, the word on the effectiveness of the cyanide gas came in as well.
The bodies of dead animals lay all about in the open. The Germans, on
the other hand, were stacked liked cordwood inside the entranceways to
the tunnels, as those inside had raced to get out while those outside had
simultaneously raced to get in.

French infantry was advancing up alongside them, creating mixed
emotions. On the one hand, it was always comforting to have added support. On the other hand, infantry and artillery only tolerated each other
and this was French infantry to boot, so that didn't make things any easier.
Most Doughboys didn't have much love for the "Froggies," who seemed
to have had most of their fighting spirit beaten out of them after four
years of war. The French, for their part, didn't hold most American fighting units in high regard, with the Marines and the Army's 1st Infantry
Division being about the only exceptions.

Even without the Germans the landscape was very dangerous. The
smell of phosgene gas—a rotting wood stench—hung heavy in the air; the
mud was so soft that field guns and wagons sank deep into it. Len watched
his step. All this made him think of previous warnings of how the earth
literally swallowed up men and equipment.

As usual, it was well after midnight on September 14th when they
reached their destination, the only advantage being that the area was
wooded and quiet. Pickets were positioned out front to keep a careful eye,
but the guns were not unlimbered and the men were allowed to sleep,
which Len did without hesitation.

Awaking in the early morning, Len couldn't help but think—so far, so
good. They had watched a four-hour bombardment at the outset of the
battle followed by a rolling barrage to support the advancing infantry—all

this without counter fire from the enemy's artillery. The rest of that first day and the following had been spent moving up, again, without counter fire from the enemy. Now, they were in a forested area at Nonsard in relative peace. Maybe the whole damn war would be this way and the Germans would run all the way back home and surrender.

The 14th was like a day off. The stable crews had finally caught up and Len gave Annabel a careful once over, paying special attention to her teeth and hooves. There was considerable debris under her shoes and he cleaned them thoroughly with a blade. He was glad to see the old nag. Horses in France weren't much, but he had grown fond of her.

The evening was one for frayed nerves. First, an officer rode into camp in near hysterics. Riding about in the dark, he and his mount had come close to becoming victims of the mud. Next, some Austrian officer, who had gone unseen by the infantry mopping up the woods after the battle, was apparently shell-shocked and randomly firing off an artillery piece (German 77mm) from his old battery. The shrapnel shells were bursting far too high to do any harm but the infantry had to go out and round him up.

It was back to work the following day. After an early breakfast, the order to mount was given, followed by the yell of "Forward—Yoh!" The column headed out from the woods at Nonsard in a westward direction to a wooded position outside Heudicourt, some 25 kilometers away. Len and the other scouts dumped their heavy artillery compasses and some of their other related equipment. It was obvious they were of little value; binoculars, a pocket compass, and a map were all they needed to direct artillery fire.

Len appreciated his current circumstances. The roads were muddy but clear of traffic congestion and he had Annabel to do his walking for him. It was almost leisurely—too leisurely. Sergeant "Fuzzy" Fleming came up alongside him and snapped him back into reality. "Come on Fairfield," he said. "This isn't a pleasure ride. Pick up the pace and keep your eyes pealed." Though Len hated to do it, he gave Annabel a jab with his spurs and she speeded up to a steady trot.

Heudicourt was largely undamaged, but the civilians remained inside and unwelcoming as the column passed through town. Battery A arrived at the woods just south of town (after midnight as usual) and pulled their equipment and mounts into the tree line for cover. Time to crawl up into the brush again and sleep.

They were in the woods near Gironville well to the west of St. Mihiel, and that had Len and everyone else puzzled. The Germans had fallen back rapidly and the Allied victory at St. Mihiel could hardly have been more one sided. It seemed the logical move was to head east in pursuit.

Even among the lowest ranks it was generally accepted as a given that after victory at St. Mihiel, the American objective would be to head east, deeper into Lorraine, and seize Metz. This would be a huge blow to the Germans, as it would deprive them of a major source of coal and no small amount of industry. It would also make the Americans the first Allied troops to enter Germany proper and capture a major city.

The Alsace-Lorraine Province had been seceded by France to Germany after the former's defeat in the Franco-Prussian War of 1870–71. Many historians would later argue that after four long years of bloody conflict, the French and their British allies were not about to allow the newly arrived upstart Americans to claim the credit as the first Allied troops to enter Germany and "win" the war. In their defense, some current historians have put forth the argument that had Pershing been allowed to drive his First Army toward the fortress city of Metz, he would have endured the same bloody stalemate that stalled George Patton's Third Army for three months some 26 years later in the autumn of 1944.

Military historian James H. Hallas, author of *Squandered Victory,* hotly contests this scenario and asserts that Metz was unprepared and, had the Americans been allowed to press their advantage after their victory at St. Mihiel, the war could have ended weeks earlier with numerous lives, on both sides, being saved. He lays the blame squarely on the French and British command whose pride prevented them from allowing the Americans to win the battle that probably would have won the war.

This was all beyond Len's current knowledge and circumstances. He was a Pfc and would go and do as he was told. The generals and politicians would make those decisions. He might hate and curse them for it but there was nothing he could do to change it.

Despite the one-sidedness of the Battle of St. Mihiel, there was no doubt that the artillery had done its job. Brigadier General Henry Todd, commanding the 58th FAB, received a letter from Campbell King, the chief of staff of the 1st Infantry Division, which Todd published in General Orders No. 10 on September 15th. It read:

> The Division Commander desires me to express to you and all of the officers and men of the 58th Field Artillery Brigade his commendation of your gallant conduct in the recent operations against the St. Mihiel salient. The loyalty and devotion it exhibited in moving forward your batteries over the most difficult country under the worst weather conditions are worthy of the best traditions of the field artillery. The skill and efficiency with which the guns were served are evidences of the high standard that obtains in the Brigade.

It was obvious the infantry appreciated finding most of the enemy dead upon their arrival on the scene, and the cyanide gas shells delivered en masse on Mont Sec by the 58th FAB had certainly accomplished this for the 1st Division, as well as the French II Colonial Corps.

There were no rolling kitchens at Gironville, so Len enjoyed a serving of hot beans, heated by burning gun cotton, and a tin of willy. The use of roads required the unit's moving at night to avoid detection and the retaliation that would surely follow from German artillery and planes. They moved out just before 7:00 a.m. on September 16th for St. Julien. Despite their caution, a German plane appeared and strafed their column while dropping some aerial bombs. Guardian angels must have been working overtime because no one was hit.

They crossed the Meuse River at Pont-sur-Meuse and Annabel snorted and hesitated as if sensing danger. Len spurred her and yanked the reins and she continued across. "Damn nag," he thought. "Don't make me any more nervous than I already am."

Well after midnight they reached the Forêt des Koeurs where they once again dismounted and moved the guns and horses into the cover of the tree line. Again, time to crawl amongst the wet, cold shrubs and sack out. As he pulled his blanket up around him, Len wondered where they were headed. It was obvious there would be another big battle somewhere—

only this time the Germans would be ready and in a much better position than they were at St. Mihiel.

What Len couldn't have known at the time was that he and almost all of the American Expeditionary Force were headed up toward the Argonne Forest. The German General Georg von der Marwitz and his Fifth Army would in fact be there en masse with as many as 44 divisions ready and waiting for their American opponents—roughly twice the strength that they had further north facing the British and their Commonwealth allies. This climatic encounter would become known as the Battle of the Meuse-Argonne and, even after almost a century later, it would remain the single deadliest battle in American history.

First contact — St Mihiel
not much danger for Len,
but first time observing in combat
Observers barage, no enemy things

. . . .

CHAPTER 7

The Lull Before the Storm

AGGIE AND LEN HAD been forced by circumstance to say their goodbyes to one another only hours after their wedding. Len was off to army training and then France, while Maggie would remain at her Western Union job in Chicago. Maggie had boundless energy and was always one to put the needs of others ahead of her own— she would never be content to spend her personal time only writing letters and crying. She did do those things, of course, along with a daily rosary and frequent visits to the church to light a candle for Len's protection, but she was driven to do far more.

Maggie had already helped the war effort more than most by turning in a draft dodger, but she wanted to do something for those truly hurting. Governor Lowden had established the Woman's Committee of Illinois State Council of Defense (SCD) in November of 1917. It was the state arm of the Woman's Committee of the Council of National Defense. These two councils were combined into the Illinois Woman's Committee (IWC). The group was organized in Chicago along the boundaries of the city's political wards.

The IWC was led primarily by Protestant society women who had more than ample amounts of time and money to spend on most anything they wanted. Before the war, they had been involved in reform movements and social justice causes straight from the progressive agenda of the era.

Maggie was in sympathy with certain things they advocated, such as women's suffrage, children's health care, and honest government in Chicago (the last an obvious oxymoron), but she did not support prohibition and found it hypocritical that their crusades to end bigotry against various groups did not seem to extend to Catholics. *boohoo - - -*

She regarded many of the leading women as nothing more than do-gooders motivated primarily by guilty consciences caused by idle wealth. Their activities gave them a chance to be seen, earn public and media praise, and obtain a certain feeling that their luncheons and galas were truly accomplishing something. The war, however, changed things somewhat.

Maggie, rather than being used in peacetime, would use the IWC to assist those in need as a result of the war. She had an organization that she could assist but not join, that would provide her with an opportunity to do the type of charitable works that came naturally to her. Women whose husbands were in military service, especially those with small children, were among those who really touched her heart. Those widowed and orphaned by the war broke it. She wanted to help them in any way possible.

The coal shortage during the winter of 1917–18 left many in dire straights. Maggie went through the neighborhood and created a list of those suffering from the cold, which she submitted to the ward leader of the IWC. Some were helped, but she felt the relief was paltry.

Drives for war bonds and food conservation programs were the major functions of the IWC. Maggie considered such efforts primarily for show, as those were things that society women could afford to do. The reality was that the vast majority of Chicago's population was lower middle class and poor. How could they afford to buy bonds or conserve food when many of them went hungry? Maggie felt it was ridiculous for the well off to finger waggle at the less fortunate about such things. Instead, she assisted in more unofficial activities: packaging books donated to soldiers from the Chicago Public Library, assisting food pantries with packages for the hungry, delivering food and medicines to flu victims quarantined in their homes, and rolling bandages for soldiers. The latter activities involved work primarily with the American Red Cross. Maggie never lacked courage or drive, and would do whatever she could for her man as well as for the wives and children who had men in the same circumstance as her Len. That was Maggie, and she was known and loved for it.

Across the Atlantic it was September 17th, and Len and the rest of the

presumably it was the same date on both sides of the Atlantic —

124th were encamped near the little village of Nicay. There were no orders to move in the morning and the supply of donuts was so plentiful that everyone was taking extras to save as a future treat or emergency ration, depending on what one's future circumstance might be. The boredom of war was upon them. The only activity was to watch the passing trains traveling back and forth through the town.

The next day the column fell out and moved into Seracourt. Len and Al discussed the current news from the rumor mill, which indicated they were headed north to the Argonne Forest for a major fight. "Wadda ya think Len?" Al asked. "Are we gonna have to mix it up?" Len shrugged. "I suppose we're due," he answered. "All this movement has to be leading us somewhere. The Heinies are licked but they just don't know it. I just wish they'd give it up. I don't want to have to kill any kids." Al nodded in agreement, "Me too."

At Seracourt there were no woods, and since camp had to be set up in an open area, a protective perimeter had to be established around the guns and wagons. On September 19th the brigade moved into the woods around Waly. "This will be the jump-off spot," Sergeant Fleming said to the men of Battery A. "We'll move on them from here when the word comes." Len had no complaints when the next morning came and went without any word to move.

Once it was obvious the 20th would be another idle day, Len asked Al and a couple of others if they wanted to wander over to a nearby farm and see if they couldn't get some fresh eggs. They were well behind the lines so they could move freely across an open field. "Hey, does anybody speak any French?" One of them asked. "We'll get our message across somehow," Len said. "Just how are we gonna do that?" Al asked. "I'll think of something. I don't want to leave without eggs," Len replied. As the four men approached the farmhouse, they saw a very attractive young woman in her early twenties carrying a small basket of chicken feed. "Bon jour, Mademoiselle!" Len said with a wide smile. "Bon jour," she responded pleasantly.

"Nous (we), aahh nous," Len repeated while waving his index finger around himself and his comrades as he struggled in vain to think of anything else he could say in French. "Aahh!" He proclaimed in triumph as he raised his finger straight up, "I've got it!" He squatted down and put his hands under his armpits with his elbows pointing out. He then began to flap his arms like wings and squawked as he strutted about. "Come on you guys," he demanded. "Help me out." The other three followed Len's lead as the obviously amused young woman watched the four Doughboys squawk and strut with great vigor.

Just to be certain she understood what they wanted, Len began to grunt and squat as if he were trying to lay an egg. The others followed suit. This went on for a minute or two before the pretty young mademoiselle could bear it no longer and, gushing with laughter, said, "Do you gentleman want eggs?" in perfect English.

A wave of embarrassment swept over the men whose faces blushed redder than radishes. "Yes ma'am," One of them said. "That would be very nice, thank you." The woman went into the hen house and returned with eight beautiful white eggs.

"My name is Janette and I would normally sell these eggs at market," she said. "But I am happy to give two eggs each to my brave American friends." The men rushed forward with repeated sighs of "merci, merci" as they collected the eggs. Despite their insistence, the woman refused their offer to pay for the eggs and sent them on their way.

"Great work Fairfield," one of them said as they left. "You really handled that with ease." "Yeah," another said. "That was sure impressive. I had no idea you had such command of the French language." Len could only blush and shrug. "Well, at least we got fresh eggs." Al threw his arm over Len's shoulders and the four of them laughed all the way back to camp.

The twigs and brush in the camp area were too wet to burn, but that didn't stop them. The scouts, like all good artillerymen, always carried some gun cotton for cooking rations. The smell of horses, coffee grounds, and horse manure permeated everything, so the four men could enjoy their freshly cooked eggs unnoticed in their own little corner of the camp.

The next day was uneventful until the sun started to go down and the order came to mount up, followed by another order, barked down the line, "We're moving out!" The destination was to the northeast on high ground overlooking the Bertraine Farm. They were near Parois just northeast of Neuvilly and this was, in times past, very much the frontline.

As Len was moving to the communications dugout to report in, he was amazed at the sight of the military fortifications around him. The dugouts were not mere holes surrounded by sandbags with lumber strewn across the top, but were deep, well constructed, heavily fortified, and watertight! There were telephone lines running everywhere. And the ammunition was not simply stacked in a ditch and covered with camouflage netting hastily thrown over, but in real shelters made of corrugated iron ("elephant iron" to the Americans, "wrinkly tin" to the Brits). The casemates' housing and camouflage covering the artillery pieces were permanent. These were the signs of static warfare and well-entrenched armies.

Len was awed by the maze of interlocking trenches that allowed men to move about with relative ease from dugout to dugout, or from one trench to another. There were even signposts on the trench walls to prevent anyone from losing their sense of direction. The trench floors had duckboard, and the artillery placements had real wooden bottoms.

Things there were quiet except for the Germans' "old-pop-in-a-barrel," which was probably a trench mortar on rails. It fired a starburst shell every so often illuminating the night sky over no man's land. Well-lit lines are easier to defend, so "old pop" was making its contribution to keeping the lines static. In fact, the area was so static that there had been little fighting in it since the war started four years earlier. It was the epitome of the "live and let live" philosophy. That would all change soon enough.

In the morning, Len saw Sergeant Fleming in a rare idle moment. "Sergeant, what's new from the grapevine?" he asked. "Not much Fairfield, the 91st Division is just north of us in Avocourt so it stands to reason if there's any trouble that's who we'll be supporting. We'll know soon enough; just watch for the red and green rockets. If they go off, then you and Slowey will go to work."

That night there were no rockets, but an order to move north toward Avocourt. It looked like there might be trouble after all. The air was cool and there was a slow drizzle that added to the men's general discomfort. To their great consternation it was discovered that the camouflage netting was left behind at Nonsard.

At first there was some confusion over what was to be done. Without camouflage netting, the artillery pieces could not be placed in wherever their new location was to be. As if by divine intervention, the 124th's new regimental commander, Colonel Horatio Hackett, rode up, having been inspecting the lines. Hackett had just been promoted from lieutenant colonel to full colonel, assuming command after the regiment's previous commander, Colonel Gordon Strong, contracted influenza in mid-September and nearly died. Strong would make a full recovery and later be reassigned to a reserve corps.

"What's the delay here?" Hackett demanded. "Our netting is back in Nonsard, sir," one of the gun crew responded. "Then you'd better take the nets from these positions," the colonel answered. "You won't have any natural camouflage where you're going." Lieutenant Casey was deferential but quick to point out that this would leave the positions they were currently vacating open to aerial observation by the enemy and subsequent bombardment. "Forget it," Hackett said. "In two days the Front is going to be thirty miles from here and these positions won't be good for anything but flower beds."

The netting was stripped and the column proceeded toward Avocourt. The Germans knew that American forces were being concentrated near the Argonne and there were frequent barrages back and forth along the frontlines. Len could feel his heart sink down to his knees, and suddenly he wasn't nearly so concerned about what age any of the enemy might be.

All of a sudden, cries of "iron cigars!" and "G.I. cans!" reverberated through the ranks as artillery shells began to fall amongst the regiment. Len jumped off Annabel and pulled her by the reins to the wagon immediately in front of him. He wrapped the reins quickly around the back of the wagon bed and then ran like the wind for a communication's trench. He sank in up to his knees and stayed there until the firing stopped. This was his first time under direct fire and he knew the wetness in the crotch of his pants was not from the rain or mud. Despite his lack of bloodlust, Len was consoling himself with the thought of returning the favor.

The only dry areas were under the wagons. Len curled up under the back of a wagon with his trousers mud encrusted from the knees down and urine soaked around the width of his pelvis. He couldn't have felt more uncomfortable as he pulled a blanket over himself. Al was on the ground lying right above him. "Nighty, night dear," Al muttered. "Goodnight and go to hell Al!" Len snapped, and with that he went unconscious from exhaustion.

Just before 6:00 am, Fuzzy was moving along the wagon lines. "Get up, you sorry sods, there's work to be done. Get up!" Everyone scrambled into formation. "There's coffee and oatmeal at the rolling kitchen," Fuzzy said. "Get some and then grab a spade. Move to it!" Len and the others hurried to grab something and then moved quickly to begin the day's work. Everyone would be digging.

By late afternoon, they had a dugout complete with functioning telephone system, unpacked shells piled high, and an operational "sewer"; the field guns were not dug, but were placed, albeit far too close together for safety. By 4:00 o'clock that afternoon they actually had time to clean up, which for Len meant washing his pants, socks, shirt and putties (leggings) in a barrel of water.

Len looked a sight with his boots on, his naked, hairy, and short legs followed by his undershorts, undershirt, helmet, and a cigarette dangling from his lips. Sergeant Fleming offered a word of encouragement. "Fairfield," Fuzzy said. "The can-can girls ain't got a thing on ya." Len glanced upward from his chore. "Why thank you sergeant," he quipped. "But don't get any ideas, I'm a married man."

His laundry complete, Len joined the others in shaving off his body hair, including the area around his equator. Everyone had to apply the anti-mustard gas paste (alkaline) that was supposed to protect skin from blistering. Len felt more uncomfortable than he had wearing the urine soaked pants.

Len and the other scouts were brought into the telephone dugout for a briefing. "There's going to be a big push all through the Argonne," they were told. "Our barrage starts at 02:30 on the 26th. It will last for precisely three hours and then halt exactly at zero hour, 05:30. The infantry jumps off right at that moment—no delays." Everyone looked at the map strewn across the table.

"You'll have one final briefing here before things start," the lieutenant continued. "The plan is to have you move up about 400 yards ahead of the batteries. The signal corps people will be in place up ahead waiting for you. They've just finished testing the service buzzers and they're fully operational." The lieutenant pointed to a marking on the map just ahead of their dugout. "Fairfield and Slowey," he said. "You'll be positioned here in the center." He then assigned the other two teams of scouts to their right and left.

They were about to participate in what would become known to history as the "Meuse-Argonne Offensive." It would open on September 26th and last right up until the exact moment that the Armistice of November 11th went into effect. Spanning 47 days, it would be one of the longest battles in American history. It would involve more than 1.2 million Doughboys, of whom more than 26,000 would die, giving it the highest American death toll of any battle in all the annals of U.S. military operations.

CHAPTER 8

The Argonne: Let the Slaughter Commence

L EN AND THE OTHER scouts were called into the telephone dugout at around 11:00 o'clock on the morning of September 25th.
Everyone had been busy readying equipment and it was obvious
something would start soon. Maps for the entire Verdun Sector, from the
Meuse River to the Argonne Forest, were spewed across the table. Field
Orders #7 were reviewed. The 58th FAB was assigned to the V Corps with
orders specifying that they would be providing artillery support to the
91st Infantry ("Wild West") Division when they jumped off the following day.

The 58th FAB was positioned to the rear of the 91st Division in the
Hesse Forest (Forêt de Hesse) at a point roughly midway between Avocourt
and what had once been Vauquois. Vauquois was now an uninhabited pile
of rubble known simply as the "Lost Village" (le village disparu). Partially
rebuilt, the 2007 census records fewer than 30 residents.

The artillery would be expected to move up quickly in support of a
rapid infantry advance. The field guns would open up at 2:30 a.m. on the
26th with a three-hour barrage of the enemy lines. Two regiments from
the 58th FAB, the 122nd and Len's 124th, would provide light artillery
support from their 75mm guns in an effort to breach enemy wire entan-
glements. The 123rd would provide the heavy artillery support with their
155mm Howitzers to demolish enemy trenches, machine guns nests, and
other strong points.

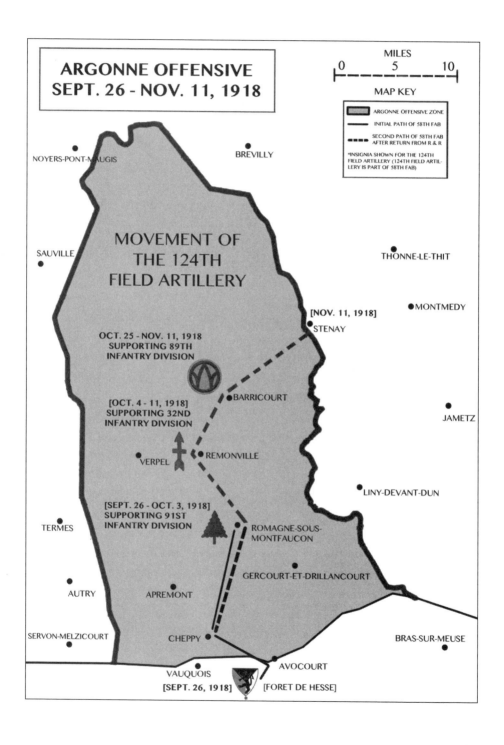

The 91st Infantry would jump off at 5:30 am, advancing under the cover of a rolling barrage that would take them all the way to Bois de Very. Len and the rest of Battery A were in the first battalion of the 124th and would be assigned to the right flank of the light artillery sub-group supporting the 181st Brigade of the 91st Division. This assignment put them under the command of Colonel Milton Foreman instead of their own Colonel Hackett. Hackett would be covering the left flank in support of the 182nd Brigade.

The plans were detailed and very specific. In addition to watching for enemy muzzle flashes, the scouts were expected to keep a careful eye on the progress of the barrage. There would be a few brief pauses in the artillery fire, long enough to let the infantry engage the surviving enemy and secure their positions, but these respites were to be brief, lasting only for periods ranging from 10 to 25 minutes.

"Questions?" asked the captain. "Will any gas shells be used, sir?" someone asked. "Yes, aerial reconnaissance has placed the German guns. They'll be shelled for about five minutes during the initial barrage about an hour before the 91st jumps off," the captain replied. "Sir, will we have engineers with us to evaluate the roads before calling for displacement of the guns?" Len asked. "There will be engineers present with your scouting teams but there will be an artillery officer present as well," the captain replied. "Only he can authorize the batteries to move forward."

"Any other questions?" the captain asked. There was silence. "Alright," the captain said. "Keep this in mind: this isn't going to be like St. Mihiel. The Heinies are well entrenched and fully expecting an attack. There's nowhere for them to fall back to. They know that taking this ground will put us on the Hindenburg Line with our next push being into Germany itself, so they're goanna fight like devils. Stay sharp and be ready. Review your maps, check your gear, check your mounts, and get everything in order. That's all—dismissed!"

Len and Al left the dugout together without saying a word. "I'm going to check on Annabel," Len said once outside. Both of them knew he was looking for something to occupy his mind as the countdown to H-Hour approached. A simple philosophy—carry out your routine and hope everything goes well. Annabel was, of course, fine. Len envied her ignorance of the danger that would soon be upon them both. He looked over his gear, again, in a matter of minutes. His sidearm was loaded and ready, binoculars, compass, map, signal flags, whistle, gas mask, gas ointment, pencil, and sketchbook. Everything was ready and waiting just as it had been when he checked it earlier. Len's routine was interrupted by a welcome treat, a rolling kitchen had arrived at midday and was serving lunch. He got in line.

After lunch Len pulled out some YMCA stationary and wrote Maggie a letter. Then he took the rosary from his pocket and said his beads. The rest of the day passed in a blur. At midnight they were ordered to report to their respective batteries. Every battery commander had a megaphone ready to shout orders to his gunners.

In preparation for rapid movement, the guns were placed in echelon (diagonally), a move that is always dangerous since it leaves them uncomfortably close together. A lucky shot from an enemy gun or a muzzle-burst from one of your own, and the entire battery can become a casualty. As at St. Mihiel, the initial responsibility of every scout would be to simply view the action while keeping a careful eye out for enemy muzzle flashes. The difference this time would be that the scouts would move out behind the infantry, watching and reporting on the rolling barrage as it progressed toward the enemy.

Al was with the battery crew waiting for Len. When he arrived they nodded at each other and hunkered down. They glanced at their wristwatches and watched as H-Hour approached. At 2:29 a.m. the battery commander raised his right hand with index finger extended, signaling one minute. He stared intently at his watch and sixty seconds later clenched his right hand into a fist and thrust it downwards. The guns immediately opened up and the silence of a few seconds earlier was shattered as French and American batteries let loose fire from a combined total of just under 4,000 artillery pieces all along the line.

The volley of fire was deafening and Len's ears rang so intensely that he couldn't distinguish any sounds other than the roar of the cannons. Soon the firing became rhythmic, and the ringing was unnoticeable as his ears adjusted to the boom—boom—boom of the cannons. This went on for three hours and at 5:30 a.m. it stopped, just as suddenly as it had begun.

The whistles in the infantry positions blew and the men of the 91st Division advanced toward the enemy.

Len and Al left the security of their positions to follow right behind. A rolling barrage would start in a matter of seconds, and the advancing infantry and artillery scouts had to keep pace with it. Len and Al carried red markers to drop at designated distances to help the battery commanders calculate range. Troops from the Signal Corps were moving up as well, unwinding spools of telephone wire and carrying up field phones (box buzzers) for the scouts to use for reporting on the rolling barrage.

Len had never previously been required to leave shelter and move into the battle area. Dawn was breaking and while a moderate rain had ceased, the area was obscured by morning fog and battle smoke. The ground was a mixture of muddy goo and shell holes. It was an atmosphere that felt as eerie as it looked and Len felt all too vulnerable. Len and Al witnessed their first combat deaths as they watched men of the 91st fall from German machine gun fire.

The rolling barrage then began, and this only added to Len's fears. The 75mm guns were dropping shells that advanced 25 meters ahead of the infantry. This was to continue to ranges exceeding 7,000 meters! Since the 75s had barrels that could not elevate for that range, the guns had to be manually propped up. This was not scientific or overly precise. A gun slipping from whatever it was resting on could easily drop a shell short and fall directly on any of their heads. Len and Al didn't know it, but Battery D had already suffered four casualties from a muzzle-burst, while another of their men had lost his left hand when he caught it under the rollers of the loading tube of a 75mm propped almost straight up.

Len dropped a distance marker when he and Al spotted a signalman waving them over. Al cranked up the phone while Len put on the headset. "Team One to Battery A," Len yelled into the mouthpiece. The appropriate corporal in the telephone dugout answered. "This is Battery A, report Team One."

"Barrage fire accurate but not wholly effective," Len stated. "Infantry advance encountering pockets of resistance from machine gun emplacements. Enemy muzzle flashes spotted from Mountfaucon at our two o'-clock."

There was a pause as if the corporal on the other end was writing down what he said or consulting with an officer. Then he came back on the line. "Affirmative Team One, the infantry will have to neutralize the remaining machine guns, proceed forward, continue watch for enemy muzzle flashes, and report when able—out!" Len removed the headset and handed it back to the signalman. "We've got to keep going Al," he said. "They want us to stay with the infantry and watch for German guns."

By 10:00 a.m. the fog burned off and the guns stopped. The infantry held up to catch their breath and regroup. They had moved ahead of the point where the artillery could effectively cover their advance and had to wait for the guns to be limbered and brought forward. The 181st Brigade's objective that first day was the heights northwest of Gesnes, an incredible distance of 14 kilometers from their jumping off point. It was obvious that between the pockets of German resistance holding out and the time required for the field guns to move up, that they'd never make it. That was good news for Fritz who would have time to regroup and re-establish his defensive positions.

Len looked all about the area and was unnerved by the dead lying just ahead of him on the field. Before this his encounters with dead soldiers had been passing their covered bodies as either he or their handlers were moving very quickly past one another on the roads. It was a frightful sight, one that made him think of just how loose the current conditions made his grip on life.

The troops of the 91st Division moved past Epinonville and into the woods. Len and the others lamented the fact that traffic jams were holding up their artillery columns. They started to finally link up at Avocourt to the right of where they should have been, in the vicinity of the 37th Infantry Division.

Len had been told soon after his first talk with French troops that he'd never forget when and where he was when he saw his first dead. They were right. It was September 26, 1918 right outside Avocourt, and it sickened him. The horror was only just beginning.

In the sky above, a German plane ducked out of a cloud and attacked an American observation balloon. The bullets from the plane's guns quickly ignited the hydrogen filled contraption and the observer leapt from its basket. His parachute opened with the huge burning hulk falling rapidly over his head and speeding downward to engulf him. The enemy plane swooped in and finished the doomed man with a burst from its guns. Whether it was an act of mercy or deliberate murder only the pilot knew, but the thousands of Doughboys on the ground who witnessed it shrieked with cries of anger, obscenities, and desires for vengeance.

Meanwhile, the men of the 91st were still advancing and encountering stiffer and stiffer resistance from the Germans, especially from their machine guns. The artillery could do nothing to help them. It was clogged in the traffic jam on the road running through the ruins of what was once Avocourt. Something had to be done, so the officers doubled the number of horses (12 instead of the usual 6) hooked to each gun carriage and ordered the men to assist the animals in getting the artillery up and over the mud pie of Avocourt Hill and the rickety bridges overlaying its trenches. Len, Al, and any man whatsoever took part in the herculean effort. They started at dawn on the 27th and didn't accomplish the task until noon.

There, just ahead of them, lay the Argonne Forest. It was a smoldering conglomerate of shattered trees, barbed wire, and colorless landscape. It looked like the entranceway to hell. Ironically, the forest was occupied by an enemy whose back was against the wall and would fight like cornered animals to defend it. Len took out his binoculars and scanned the area ahead when it started to rain. "How appropriate," he muttered to himself.

Reconnaissance reports were coming in from the Very-Chappy crossroads, and they weren't good. Apparently, it was a complete cluster fuck. Three American infantry divisions were all snarled up at the crossroads and unsure of which direction to proceed. There was still no artillery support to speak of, and the Germans were having a field day killing Americans. Rumors were circulating that the enemy would counterattack and route the Doughboys. Len and every man in the unit were itching to do anything to help.

The MPs decided that desperate measures called for desperate actions. They ordered everything but the artillery pieces and ammunition wagons off the road even if it meant dumping ambulances into ditches. All priority was to be given to the field guns.

Len threw his haversack into a pile with the others. It was 3:00 o'clock in the afternoon and they had four guns, a full battery, moving up the road with ammunition. The fleeing enemy had sabotaged the bridges over the trenches, but that didn't deter the men in their rescue effort. They unhitched the horses and pulled the caissons themselves over makeshift planking. By 5:00 o'clock they had the guns at the Very-Chappy crossroads.

Colonel Hackett, a modern day Stonewall Jackson, was standing in full view of his troops as well as those of the enemy, ignoring the potential danger from German machine guns and artillery, directing men and the placement of guns. Hackett was revered by every man in the regiment.

Two guns were being placed in an area that just hours ago had been used by the Germans for their own field guns. This was all being done under the watchful eye of two enemy observation balloons. Len was getting ready to move forward to scout, when he overheard a panicked voice on the other end of a signalman's phone: "Raise the distance of your artillery fire, for God's sake you're killing our own men!" The poor bastard obviously didn't know that the American guns had not yet started firing. The infantry was being shelled by the enemy.

Len and Al had no idea where their horses were and so the two of them began to race ahead on foot. Along the way, they heard from signalmen that the 91st had advanced so far so fast that they had outpaced their flanks. The 37th Division on their right and the 35th on their left were far behind. This meant the 91st had created a salient in the enemy lines and was now catching fire from the Germans on three sides.

There were more observation teams than batteries available, but together they had the location of the German positions ahead of the 91st and around midnight directed a barrage against them that lasted almost half an hour. There were no cries of friendly fire this time and the bombardment seemed to keep the Heinies at bay.

By noon on the 28th the Germans had 150mm guns shelling the American artillery positions, requiring them to displace immediately and move their crews and their pieces forward yet again. Miraculously, none of the American guns were hit in the mêlée, but the 124th had some fresh dead in the ditches alongside the day-old corpses from the 91st. Len, Al, and other observers were on the outskirts of Very when their guns caught up to them. Like Avocourt, Very was a wreck. There were makeshift aid stations set up amongst the smoldering wreckage and men were laid out everywhere. They seemed to be dying by the second.

There was no time to rest. The observers and batteries were ordered to continue forward toward Epinonville. German 77mm guns were dropping shells on them as they advanced. Len wished he had Annabel but it seemed his feet carried him just as quickly as she could. The road was deemed too dangerous to stay on and the men and guns were ordered off of it. One of the officers yelled out an order for everyone to grab whatever was available for digging. The guns would have to be placed right where they were and everyone could only pray they wouldn't be blown to bits before they could return fire.

Everyone was scared plenty, and it didn't help matters when word came down that evening that Colonel Hackett had his jaw taken off by shrapnel, accompanied by a significant chest wound. Len and everyone else wondered—if Hackett could get it, who was safe?

That evening, everyone was working furiously to dig the trail pits for the guns, when a horrific rain started. "Lord, please help us; don't work against us," Len prayed silently to himself. He removed his helmet and bailed out the hole he was digging. He hardly had time to remove a few shovels full of earth when the hole filled with water again. This was followed by the discovery of solid rock just a foot or so down. It seemed the guns would never be placed. "God, are you trying to tell me something?" Len asked in more silent prayer. No food, no warmth, no rest, and no end to the German shells falling around them. "Lord, just let it be quick," Len thought. Still, Len was grateful. The infantry from the 91st Division was barely a half-mile ahead of them, and they were catching hell from the Germans' fire. There was always somebody worse off.

The morning brought an end to the rain, and the artillery fire had stopped during the night. The guns were now in place and had an effective range of two miles. Soon it would be time to reciprocate the Germans with a barrage.

Len and Al lined up by the rolling kitchen for a hot breakfast. A dead German lay alongside but nobody seemed to care. "Major (Frank) Rearden's taken command," the cook said to Len as he filled his mess. It seemed like cooks, and anyone other than those most impacted by the news, always had the latest word on everything. Passing it on seemed to give them a feeling of importance. "Well," Len said. "I hope he's a damn site luckier than poor Hackett."

Len and Al were sitting along the road finishing breakfast when Sergeant Fleming approached them. "You two will form team two and head up the road roughly a thousand yards to the infantry. The signalmen will have phones waiting. Scout out the lines and call in the precise coordinates of the enemy back here to the battery, " Fleming said. Len and Al dumped the remainder of their breakfast on the ground and got up to go. "And watch yourselves," the sergeant added. "The Heinie machine guns are spraying fire everywhere."

The supply wagons hadn't arrived yet with their packs (which contained most of their equipment) so they started out with just their side arms on their belt, their maps in their pocket, and their binoculars around their necks. "Len, why the hell did they even bother giving us horses?" Al asked. "We never get a chance to ride the damn things." Len grinned. "Because Al," Len said. "It doesn't make any sense, so that's what you have to expect the army to do."

As the two men neared the front, the chatter from the machine guns was deafening, and they could hear bullets whizzing around them. They hunkered low as they looked for a good spot to view the enemy lines. A corporal spotted the two of them moving along the rear of the lines. At first he thought he might have spotted some stragglers and was going to box their ears, but the artillery Pfc stripes (crossed cannons) on their arms and the binoculars around their necks made it obvious what they were all about.

The corporal ran over to them crouched down. "You two need a place to scout things out?" he yelled over the machine gun fire. "We sure as hell do," Len yelled back. "The 37th is on the other side of that hill to our right," said the corporal. "Half way up that ought to give you a damn good view of the German lines." Len nodded and tapped Al on the shoulder as the two spotted a signalman to take along.

They scurried up to the halfway point of the hill, knowing that enemy snipers would be watching for just such a move. Al put on the headset from the field phone while Len looked out at the German lines with his

Len (s' Argonne

binoculars. Before putting them to his eyes, he looked over at the men of the 37th, who were trying to advance against machine gun fire by moving over open ground with fixed bayonets. The Germans were cutting them down like wheat. Len gaped in horror. He reported the muzzle flashes from Montfaucon and from another location on his map well to the German rear. He had nothing with which to sketch the layout of the enemy trenches but reported the position of the area closest to the infantry.

Bullets started to ping uncomfortably close to the three of them. "We've done everything we can do here," Len said. "Let's get the hell outta here before they shell us," Al said. The three men moved down off the hill with extreme prejudice.

Upon their return, they learned that three enemy batteries had been taken out. Other scouting teams from the 58th FAB, as well as those from the 91st and 37th Infantry Divisions, had forwarded the same data to various commanders, so while no one could be directly credited with the kills, having the same coordinate layings coming from several different sources provided such precise information in range and deflection that the German batteries were doomed. Considering it was killing, there was a strange sense of satisfaction in a job well done.

Unfortunately, the muzzle flashes from the American guns that had rained down such destruction on the Germans had apparently been spotted by the enemy's scouts. Now it was the Americans' turn to take a hit. The Germans were dropping high velocity shells, 88mm, right on their position. These were the dreaded "whizz-bangs," so named because the shell travelled faster than the speed of sound; the "whizzing" of the shell was heard before the "bang" of the gun firing it. With no warning of incoming rounds, the result is many a man being blown to pieces before anyone becomes aware enough to realize what's happening.

After the first round hit and soldiers saw what was happening, it was bedlam as everyone scurried for a foxhole or cover of any kind. It kept up for 30 minutes while everyone hugged the ground. More than a few murmuring prayers were heard—Len among them. It stopped suddenly. At first, it seemed everyone was all right but then word starting spreading of this man or that one who had been killed. Len was glad that Annabel had missed the show. There were a lot of dead horses.

The morning breakfast line was unusually full as several stragglers from the infantry clogged up the rear. The 91st and 37th had suffered greatly, and many of these grunts were looking in vain for their officers, now mostly dead, to lead them back to their units.

Len and the others could see how precarious the situation was. In front of them the 91st was badly mauled, and was, by the accounts from their own messengers, runners and carrier pigeons, "barely hanging on." As if this wasn't bad enough, many of the artillerymen were casualties as well. There was also a need for additional shells and fuses. "It's bad Len," said Al. "It's worse than bad," Len replied. "If the Germans attack, they'll sweep us away like dust."

Someone in high command must have reasoned that the best defense is a good offense because word came down that an infantry attack against the Germans was coming in ten minutes. The word was so late that there would be no time to send the scouts out to reconnoiter the area and check coordinates. A rolling barrage was required, and all the scouts could do was observe for muzzle flashes as the guns would bombard along the area believed to be the German front lines.

The 58th FAB had 24 guns hitting the Germans for almost two hours—all for nothing. The attacking Doughboys dropped like flies in the face of enemy machine guns. The Germans stopped them cold. This was followed by horrific news. The Germans were counterattacking! They did not attack on the American right between the 91st and 37th Divisions but rather on the left between the 91st and 35th Divisions. This area was a surprise move and, whether by accident or design, a good one for the Germans since the 35th had been seriously hurt and there was something of a gap between them and the 91st. This peril was not lost on the artillery as they hurried to wheel their guns left to hit the attacking enemy. Engineers had been called up and were ready to begin destroying their own artillery pieces should the Germans break through the infantry and reach their positions.

Len, Al, and the other scouts were given rifles taken from dead American infantrymen. "You many need these," they were told as the weapons were thrown hastily to them. The directive was a simple one: do or die. If the Germans got past the infantry, any man standing was to fight to the death "to keep the enemy at bay long enough for the guns to be disabled."

The orders were for each field gun to fire one round per minute until the shells were gone. The guns opened up in the late afternoon of October 1st and were still firing past midnight. Len and some of the others had to set down their rifles and assist in fusing shells. The artillery crews were so short-handed that each gun was being manned by just a sergeant and two men. By some miracle the infantry held on, and the Germans were unable to break through the line.

Morale soared as it was announced that the First Infantry Division was on its way up to relieve the 35th. Every Doughboy in France knew that the First Division was the most experienced and combat capable division in the entire AEF. The news was sweetened by the fact that they were bringing with them their artillery unit, the 7th Field Artillery.

Like a story about cavalry riding to the rescue in a dime novel, the horse teams and caissons of the 7th FA came roaring up the road and immediately began setting up despite German shells bursting all around them. Len and the men of the 58th cheered loudly as their brothers in the 7th went about their work as calmly and professionally as if it were nothing more than a timed exercise back in the states.

The firing guns of the 7th meant that the 58th's guns could get a much-needed chance to cool down. During the previous week's fighting, the 58th FAB had provided artillery support to the 91st, 37th, and 35th Infantry Divisions and now the men and their guns needed to rest. If only the Germans had seen it that way. Whizz-bangs were still falling on their position, and Len quivered when he saw the results of a direct hit on a caisson that blew it to bits and killed eight men instantly.

It was October 3rd, a full week after the Argonne Offensive began, and Len finally had a chance to lie down and sleep. He didn't sleep as much as went unconscious from exhaustion. When he finally awoke several hours later he was hungry but decided to write Maggie a letter before getting some chow—it was a move that probably saved his life. As he wrote, Len knew that any mention of the battle would be certain to be cut out by the censors and worry Maggie to boot, so he merely said that he was doing well, that he missed and loved his beautiful bride, and looked forward to their life together.

There had been some firing by the brigade during the day without too much response from the Germans, and at around 7:00 p.m. everyone knew why. Dozens of enemy planes swooped down and began dropping bombs ("eggs"). They were damned accurate. Len threw himself into a shell hole hoping that lightning wouldn't strike twice. The bombs hit horses, caissons, and even the chow line by the rolling kitchen that Len would have been standing in if he hadn't been writing a letter to Maggie instead.

It was as if it were raining flesh and entrails. Squatting in the carnage, he vomited uncontrollably as the bombs continued to fall all around him. He tried to be optimistic, realizing that an oral purging might relieve the awful diarrhea he had been suffering from.

Machine guns and anti-aircraft fire ("Archie") lit up the sky as the enemy planes circled overhead. Soon the planes broke off and headed east. As Len climbed out of the shell hole, he looked at the bodies and wreckage all around him. He had only been in combat for a month, and already felt as if he had experienced a lifetime of war.

He watched as the fresh troops of the 32nd Infantry ("Red Arrow") Division marched past on their way to relieve the men of the 91st. On the other side of the road came the battered remnants of what was once the 91st Division as it moved toward the rear. These wonderful bastards had endured hell, been mauled almost beyond recognition, and yet still held the line despite the Germans throwing everything they had them. Len's eyes welled with tears as he watched them pass.

Despite all that had happened, the battle was far from over. Len and his comrades would need to gird their loins yet again. The next day, October 4th, would begin the second phase of the Argonne Offensive, which would result in the additional slaughter of countless thousands of Doughboys both among the infantry and the artillery.

CHAPTER 9

. . . .

Bearding the Lion in His Den

AFTER THE APPALLING casualties at the end of the battle's first week, the high command saw to it that the infantry units on the front line were relieved. The 1st Division relieved the 35th, the 91st Division was relieved by the 32nd, and the 37th and 79th Divisions were pulled from the line as well, while the 3rd Division moved up to the front. All of the fighting and dying had resulted in a mere two- to five-mile gain in ground along the various sections of the American front. Now, with a new supply of fresh troops, the offensive would enter its second phase, and the killing would not only begin anew but ramp up somewhat as well.

Len and the 58th FAB were still near Very. The 32nd Division was directly in front of them, with the First on their left and the Third on their right. The morning saw the guns firing while the newly placed infantry divisions situated themselves. Some supply wagons started to roll in, and Annabel was brought up with the mounts. It was like seeing an old friend. Len ran up to her and put his arms around her neck. "Glad to see you, you beautiful old nag," he said. He sensed that Annabel too was happy at their reunion. *New commander*

Apparently in preparation for the renewed offensive, a new commander was brought in to relieve Major Rearden. He was Colonel Joseph Rogers and was regular army all the way. His previous command was the 18th Field Artillery. Word was that he knew his business and did not shy from a fight.

The infantry was going to need added support. The guns would have to fire as far as three miles ahead (their maximum range), and this would require observation. Len knew that Annabel had been brought up for more than just companionship. It would soon be time to get to work.

That night Len was sharing a tent with Al as German artillery began to fall on their position. At first, they both seemed too tired to care and were more concerned with how they might sleep through it. Then they noticed the sound of the shells. They were landing with a dull thud or "plopping" noise. They weren't high explosives—they were gas shells! "Mustard!" Al yelled as the first whiff of fumes entered under their tent. Len and Al had their masks on in seconds. Then Len remembered—Annabel!

He ran from the tent to her and grabbed the mask from its burlap bag. While it resembled a feeding bag, every horse or mule in military service who had ever worn one was only fooled the first time. The mules and horses hated the damn things and resisted having them put on. The mask was canvas with multi layers of cheesecloth, which the animals particularly hated. Oilcloth covered the mouthpiece area to make it more palatable. Len then attached the elastic over Annabel's face which kept the mask on.

All the poison gases, but especially mustard, settled in low-lying areas like shell holes and trenches. Mustard gas reacted primarily to moisture, so while it could cause serious damage to lungs and eyes, it was more likely to come in contact with skin. This could cause severe blistering and necrosis all over the body of a soldier or animal. It has yellow color and a pungent odor, hence its name.

The next morning Len woke with a ferocious headache and to the sound of Al vomiting. He got up to help his friend but before he could approach him, Len was overtaken by nausea. He too began to vomit. It dawned on him that the German chemical barrage must have been a "cocktail," a mixture of more than one gas.

Len and most soldiers had been trained to recognize poison gases by their particular odors. Mustard Gas was easy enough to recognize, and often a soldier had ample time to put on a mask. In this case, the Germans had used arsenic gas as well. Arsenic gas smelled like geraniums, but that odor was obscured by the mustard gas. Obviously, both men had inhaled some of it in the seconds before they put on their gas masks and were now paying the price. Most soldiers recovered from mild inhalations of the various gases; even the blindness caused by mustard gas could be temporary (e.g. Adolph Hitler) if exposure was limited, but this did not mitigate the fear and misery for those not seriously or mortally wounded by such attacks.

They both decided that breakfast was out of the question. Between diarrhea and vomiting the pair were dehydrating. They knew that as soon as their stomachs allowed, they would have to get coffee down but right now it was all they could do to stand up. Len frisked himself to see if he had anything that could help. He felt something in his pocket and reached in. It was the gas ointment used on the skin for mustard burns. He looked at the tube in the palm of his hands and rolled his eyes. "What a crock of shit!" he murmured. "Please Len, don't mention shit," Al said as he bolted from the tent.

Ammunition wagons and trucks were appearing in force, so it seemed there would be no worry about supply. Things were relatively quiet except for a few brief artillery duels which were short in duration and seemed to be more of a matter of each side harassing the other than anything else.

Dysentery was running rampant through the camp, and Len was praying he wouldn't contract it. The only way for a soldier, who wasn't already doubled over in pain, to know if he had dysentery was to go through the arduous task of examining his liquid shit, mostly undigested beans, for blood. Diarrhea, dysentery, vomiting, influenza, gas, not to mention enemy shelling and aerial attacks: "Can it get any worse?" Len wondered to himself.

October 7th brought continued good news for the artillery scouts, as the static lines meant the infantry were slaughtering each other at such close range that there wasn't much role for the artillery. The occasional artillery duels were no joke—Len and Al witnessed more than a dozen men being carried to the dressing station, most looking like they wouldn't make it there alive. Also, men were having breakfast in a nearby barn when a shell burst overhead, hitting almost everyone inside with shrapnel. The new commander of Battery F was there at the time and mortally wounded. Witnesses claimed his last words were, "Take care of my men."

The next day still saw continued fighting around Epinonville Hill as more and more ammunition rolled into camp. A momentary wave of euphoria swept through the ranks when word came over from the nearby

French batteries that Germany had surrendered. The battery commanders kept firing without hesitation. The Germans returned fire and some shells started dropping in camp. "I knew it was too good to be true," Al said to Len. "So did I," Len replied. "The French are full of shit."

Len and Al saddled up in the morning on October 9th and headed toward the front lines. As they neared the 32nd Division's rear, they noticed that the infantry had moved up much further than they imagined. In fact, the 32nd would do so much damage to the Germans that the French would refer to them as, "Les Terribles." Len saw an MP enjoying a momentary respite with a hot cup of coffee and directed Annabel toward him in a slow walk.

The MP looked up as if he wanted to shoo them away. "You'll need to do your scouting up near Romagné," he said glancing up at them. "I just got back from that area. Our boys made it in and they're probably driving the Heinies out right now." That was not only good news for the infantry but for the artillery as well. Len and Al knew that Romagné would put them out of range of the 58th's guns, and that would probably mean relief unless the bastards in command decided to send them moving up again in support.

The two scouts rode further up to the sound of the fighting. As they approached, it seemed that all they were hearing was some light arms fire. When they reached the forward area they were spotted by a quartermaster sergeant who was working furiously, directing the unloading of supply crates. "Are you bringing up manure?" he asked. "Manure" was code for artillery shells when using a field phone. While code was not necessary in face-to-face conversation, it seemed soldiers always preferred referring to their situation and supplies in the most derogatory way possible.

"No," Al said. "We need to get a look at the Heinies' position." The sergeant said, "You'll have to hurry. They're on the other side of Romagné running for home." Then he pointed toward Mountfaucon. "Give us another day or two and we'll have Mountfaucon, then you can go up there and observe them all you want." That was welcome news. The two men turned their horses around and headed back to camp. Scouts and runners all along the line were reporting the same thing. The 1st and 32nd Divisions were advancing despite casualties and had the better of the fight. Rumor was that the 58th FAB was going to be on the move soon. The big question was whether that move would be forwards toward Epinonville or to the rear.

The following day everything was packed up and ready to move. There was nowhere near enough horses to move the guns up rapidly, so everyone hoped that even the brass could see it was time to move toward the rear. Word came on October 11th to head back toward Avocourt! Oh, thank God! Len thought.

No one knew it at the time, but the war's end was just one month away. Every last Doughboy realized the end couldn't be that far off, but of course, every last one of them was also hoping that it would come before they would be sent back into it. There was a gentle rain falling as the unit camped in some woods along the road. Two days in a peaceful forest was enough time to let the men catch their breath and feel some sense of tranquility.

Orders came to move out on the 14th. Len and the others soon learned they were headed to a rest camp at Brocourt commonly referred to as "Camp de Mud." It was in reality a huge mud hole situated in the middle of a mist-laden forest with crappy shacks made of tin. The only advantage it offered over the front was that there was no one shooting at them. Other than that, it was as dank, dreary, and depressing a place as one could ever hope to find. The mud was deep and thick and the horses sank anywhere from their knees to their bellies. Len brought Annabel up near the picket lines to wrap her reins around a hitching post. The two swayed and struggled to navigate through the slimy ground; she seemed more uncomfortable than Len did.

Len's bowels were in knots and he was worried. The dysentery problem was legion, and he would have to report to the aid station if he found himself joining the ranks of the ill. The medical treatment was inadequate and the disease could easily become a death sentence, especially if combined with the flu pandemic, which was at its height. Many a poor Doughboy lying flat on his back from dysentery contracted flu or pneumonia and quickly succumbed to its deadly effects.

Len was still forced to stare into his liquid shit for blood. This was no easy task as there were few latrines in the rear and none at the front. The soldiers shit on the ground, which was already mud. Since the blood from dysentery came from high in the bowels it was usually black, not an easy thing to distinguish from mud. Soldiers shit on trees, stumps, rocks, or anything else that might ease the task of fecal inspection. Though the regular inclusion of beans in their meals resulted in ever more frequent bowel evacuations, it made their examination that much easier since beans usually passed through undigested.

Coming back from the tree line after completing this ritual, Len was asked by Al how he was doing. "I'm developing quite a new perspective for shit," Len said. "What worries me is the strain it puts on my eyes," he added. "How do mean?" asked Al. "Is it affecting your vision?" Len winced as he grabbed his belly. "In a way," he replied. "I'm afraid I'm developing rectitis." Al looked puzzled. "What the hell is that? I've never heard of it." Len looked his good friend directly in the face and put his hand on his shoulder. "It's when your optic nerve droops down to your asshole and gives you a shitty outlook on life," he said. The two men laughed heartily.

The rolling kitchens were in abundance and well supplied. Still, Len kept his diet limited when possible. He ate primarily oatmeal, apples, and hardtack. Some of the officers had secured some cognac and saw to it that it was distributed to the ailing men. The NCOs dispensed it. When mixed with raw eggs it was said to cure most anything that ailed a man, especially diarrhea and flu. Len didn't care much about the basis of such a claim—he just drank his ration.

Word spread on October 16th that the 58th FAB was now part of the newly formed American Second Army. The possible meaning of such an action resulted in a set of contradictory rumors. One said that this meant the outfit would sit out the winter and not see any more action until the spring. The other meant that an American invasion of Germany was now a certainty. "Odd," Len mused to himself. "No one around here can distinguish shit from Shinola, except me of course. I've developed a real eye for shit."

Len and the others spent the day readying themselves and their equipment for an inspection on the 18th. Everyone drilled; Len and those with horses took them into a clearing to be brushed and massaged. Then, in what seemed like an act of cruelty, led them back to the mud pits for re-emersion.

That night Len and Al were sharing a tent and talking of home. Lying on his back, Len was massaging his abdomen which was finally starting to feel some relief. Things were quiet until the roar of motors overhead broke the silence of the tranquil night. "Planes!" Len yelled at Al. "And they don't sound like ours." The next moment bombs started falling around the camp and the two men bolted from their tent. They dove for cover in some ditches alongside the wagons. It lasted for an hour, but it seemed like an eternity.

When it was over everyone began to pull themselves from the muck and slime. Casualties were minimal. It seemed the surrounding woods absorbed most of the blows but Len and Al had to sleep in wet, muddy clothes. All of the following day was spent cleaning up debris and preparing their equipment and themselves for inspection. They had to look like an authentic army with real soldiers who actually gave a damn.

The following day the entire brigade was lined up with guns ready for inspection. Everyone waited in good order for an ordnance officer from the French Army to arrive and look over the guns. It didn't bode well when an American major showed up first with his shorts in a knot. He ranted and raved at the battery commanders about the mud on the guns. Obviously, no one had informed him that there wasn't enough clean water available for the men to wash and shave with let alone clean the guns.

A French general arrived with General Todd to conduct the actual inspection. It went off without a hitch, as the French general seemed far more interested in the condition of the interior of the guns' barrels than in their outward appearance. While Len was unable to make out any of the dialogue of the generals, it was clear by General Todd's large smile that things had gone well.

The next day, during a rainstorm, the 124th FA Regiment passed in review before Major General McNair. "The old man has to be happy," Len whispered to Al. "The guns get cleaned and we get our bath all while on parade—now that's military efficiency!"

On the 20th, Len and Al enjoyed an authentic day off. Rumors were still contradictory. The French papers were predicting a soon end to the awk war, but word was that the American drive in the Argonne had been stopped and that the war would continue to grind on.

The next day Len noticed his shit was relatively solid again and his gut hurt less. Lieutenant Casey brought back cigarettes from a Red Cross station in L'Aubrecourt, and life was worth living again. Len wrote Maggie and later joined in one of the poker games. The poker game was followed by a mandatory de-lousing.

Lice were primarily the worry of the infantry living in the trenches, but the harsh outdoor conditions and the lack of regular bathing were hardly conducive to avoiding the little vermin. The men usually dealt with lice by taking off their shirts and running a candle along the cloth. The lice would reveal themselves when they fled the heat, and the soldiers would catch them between their fingertips and crush them. It gave them a momentary diversion but the act was futile. It was, as the expression goes, like trying to pick fly shit out of pepper. Even worse, soldiers often unintentionally lit their shirts on fire. _gratuitous_

In 1918, military technology was applied not only to weapons but to hygiene as well. The British Foden steam powered vehicles (lorries) carried large sterilizing washers for clothing. The troops stripped down, amongst great humor, to have their uniforms de-loused, a procedure as futile as the candle method. The men were instantly re-infested as soon as they came into contact with the hay used for feeding horses or for making their own beds.

Len awoke the next morning to the sound of fresh horses being brought into camp. This was not welcomed news. It could mean only one thing: fresh horses for a fresh offensive.

Thomas Tifft, a second lieutenant, announced he had been given command of the battery. That was all right, but it was followed with news that the next day they would be headed back to the Argonne. The Argonne needed to be taken as the jump-off point for the push into Germany. It sent chills down Len's spine to think that he and everyone else had to go back. How much more could the Germans take? How many more had to die? Wouldn't this shit ever end?

The orders were barked out just after lunch on the 23rd, "Mount up! We're moving out!" Len brought Annabel up to the road and got into formation. He stroked her nose, "Well ole' girl, here we go," he said. They got only a short distance when the MPs directing traffic ordered everyone but the drivers to dismount and walk. "Al's right, why the hell does this army even bother giving us horses?" Len muttered. They reached the out-skirts of Very, the same spot they occupied before, just about midnight. It was muddier and a lot wetter than their previous stay, and the dugouts had been disassembled to make duckboards, just to maneuver around. "Home sweet home, huh Len?" Al said sarcastically. "Yeah, old friend, home sweet home," Len sighed.

The next day was spent milling about and waiting for orders. They came right after supper. The unit was assigned right back to the V Corps of the U.S. First Army and ordered to move forward up to Romagné. The stay there was momentary. On October 25th the column, some five miles long, continued on toward Mountfaucon. Amazingly, everyone was al-lowed to ride despite the close proximity of the front. The road was steep and the going slow in the dim light.

Along the way they passed a large crucifix in the road. It seemed to symbolize the men's plight. There was complete silence in the ranks. Len, and many other Catholics, blessed themselves as they passed the crucifix. So many French villages—Avocourt, Very, Romagné, and now Mount-faucon—at this moment existed only on maps. In reality they were noth-ing more than heaps of rubble, cemeteries containing only burnt ruins and dead bodies. Len could hardly imagine how deep the French desire for revenge must be and how the Germans must tremble with fear over such consequences.

The movement was slow and the column was forced to halt many times. Each halt brought a renewed sense of anxiety, as every Doughboy knew that a brisk shelling of the road would wipe out most everything, and everyone, on it. In the distance there were flashes against the dark sky as a dint echo of cannon booms wafted over the column.

The men travelled on through yet another destroyed village littered with twisted debris and surrounded by a never-ending landscape of shell holes. They were passing by the gravesites of German and American dead. It was an eerie realization that they saw before them—the unholy price paid for the back and forth ownership of such a worthless piece of ground.

Len's uneasiness was quickly dimmed by a sobering irony. Artillery probably killed many of these men. The strange oddity here was that these dead were properly buried in marked graves while other artillery fatalities are buried by the continuous barrage from the guns, only to be exhumed and then reburied yet again by still more shelling. It was a twisted reality that had to give Satan great pleasure.

The column suddenly started moving forward at a fast trot. Len and Al glanced at each other with a look of concern. It must be a move to place the guns and quickly engage the enemy, but at a crossroads, an American MP was holding up a French column to let the Doughboys pass without waiting. It was just a matter of national pride, directing traffic to prevent yet another cluster fuck. — and then he ruins it The advantage was quickly lost, though, as the first American reel cart proceeded only to cut its turn too close and get hung up on a kilometer marker along the road. The experienced French teams didn't hesitate and immediately pressed their advantage, heading straight on through the intersection ignoring the American MP who was flailing his arms in a futile motion for them to halt.

This seemed only to incite the American column, which would not be deterred. In a spontaneous act, the Doughboys drove their horses into a near fever pace as they wheeled right in a determined effort to force their allies into sharing the road. The French ranks were quickly intermingled with rowdy Americans securing space wherever it could be found.

Len and Al were not about to be left out of the melee. "C'mon Al, giddy up Annabel!" Len yelled. "Let's show the Froggies how it's done!" He spurred her and the horse bolted instantly. Len and Al swooped into file; amazingly, the skill and experience of both columns allowed the two nationalities to share the road at breakneck speed without a single accident. Then the French broke off and moved in their assigned direction. The entire thing could not have come off better if it had been rehearsed. It blew off steam for everyone involved.

A somber mood returned as the men moved into Romagné. There was no road sign denoting the town but rather a hand painted sign hung on a building. The destruction was recent and the retreating Germans had looted the town thoroughly—right down to the furniture from private homes. "What the hell is anyone going to do with a living room chair in a trench?" Len thought.

The town had just been liberated by the American 89th Infantry ("Rolling W") Division. This was the latest unit that the 58th FAB was assigned to work for. The 58th had previously supported the 1st, 91st, and then 32nd Infantry Divisions—the 89th would be their fourth and final assignment of the war.

As they moved into Romagné, Len spotted the makeshift supply depot that the 89th had established. The sounds of war were near and clearly visible in the night skies to the west and north. Len could hear high explosive shells bursting and gas klaxons banging in the near distance while watching tracer shells along the horizon, but no one in Romagné seemed to pay much notice. They passed a rolling a kitchen stopped along the road, but there was no stopping.

"Looks like another night of hardtack and willy," Al said to Len as they galloped past. "That sure whets the appetite," Len replied sarcastically. The road forked and the column moved to the left. The sign could not be discerned in the dark, but machine gun fire could be heard in the distance. That alone was enough to let them know that they were headed in the right direction.

The column moved forward onto the slope of a valley, and the batteries began to break off one by one and take up position in the muddy ground. The moon was illuminating the area, causing none too little concern among the men who were worried that the German artillery might well take advantage of the situation. "The battery is a sitting duck here Len," Al said. Len dismounted and sank knee deep in mud as he shook his head in disgust. "Yeah," he said. "Well, what else is new?"

The shells all around bore grim witness to the extensive artillery duels that had taken place in the valley and on the hill. In the morning the camouflage went up, and that seemed to create a certain degree of confidence, however illusory it might be. Len knew it didn't require an artillery scout to know that the position of this hill had been well plotted by the Germans in previous fighting, but such conditions were not new to them. They would just have to win the duel once the artillery fight commenced.

As the afternoon approached, there was no sign of the rolling kitchens or ration wagons. This would mean making due with whatever little bit of things edible the men had on them. Len had hardtack and sardines while Al had a can of tomatoes. They set up a pup tent and split their rations for dinner.

The peace of the night was shattered, not by enemy fire but by an ammunition train that had come up to re-supply the batteries. They were not combat veterans and had been severely rattled by shelling as they passed by Cierges on their way to Romagné. Romagné was even closer to the enemy, so the supply personnel were literally throwing their cases of shells and fuses from their wagons without even stopping. The cases were smashing open on a roadway filled with traffic.

Len, Al and every other artilleryman was running out demanding they stop but to no avail. The fools in the wagons obviously didn't know that the likelihood of dying from their stupidity was far greater than that posed by the enemy. The wagons disappeared into the night and there was nothing to do but clean things up and help haul the shells to their batteries.

No sooner did the shells get placed when the Germans decided to sow a little chaos of their own. Shells started to plop along the hillside. From the stench they omitted no one had to wait for the klaxon before putting on their masks—the Germans were hitting the line with mustard gas. Len and Al got the horses and went through the usual struggle of getting the animals' masks on as well as their own.

Daylight on October 26th brought no relief as the Germans stepped up the pace. Along with gas shells, they fired heavy artillery, including whizz-bangs. The results were grotesque, as once more, bits of human and animal flesh rained down about the hillside. Cries and moans from the wounded and dying filled up any vacant spaces of silence. The barrage expanded to include Romagné.

Len and Al hunkered down under a wagon. A shell landed near them, destroying a similar wagon and atomizing the horse hitched to it. Another shell landed under a moving ambulance and decapitated the driver. Still another round landed directly in a crater left from a previous shelling and the parts of both its occupants flew high into the air. The thirty minutes of shelling felt like it lasted for thirty hours. It was obvious that the Germans had saved their co-ordinates from their previous observation of the area.

The 124th's batteries were not yet prepared to counter fire, but a 155mm in the area was, and it immediately went into action for a little payback. The men grinned at each other and nodded as it roared back at the Heinies. The action of the 155 was the high point of the morning.

At around 10:30 that morning planes from a Richthofen Jasta appeared overhead. They circled about and some dropped down to fire at an American two-seater observation plane, a DH-4, without success. The action brought all the Doughboys to their feet, as every available gun in the camp was turned skyward at the German planes. Len couldn't resist joining in the ruckus and drew his Colt .45 sidearm. He knew it was a waste of time; even the anti-aircraft firing wasn't accomplishing anything, but still he popped away, almost gleefully, at the enemy overhead.

The Germans circled leisurely about, directing artillery fire with tracers fired in machine gun bursts, until their intended target, the church steeple in Romagné, was destroyed. The Germans then broke off and headed for home. The Germans would get a little more payback later in the day when the 124th fired a couple hundred gas shells into the woods just north of Bantheville.

Len and Al mused how they had now gone for two days without hot food and not much in the way of rations to boot. The kitchens and food wagons may not have gotten through, but the artillery pieces didn't seem to be bothered by any holdup. There were even coastal guns brought in and in no small quantity to be sure. It was plain for all to see that the enemy was soon to be hit with a massive amount of artillery. Len looked at the vast display of firepower being assembled and thanked God he was serving on the Allied side of the lines.

October 27th proved to be a glorious day. The rolling kitchens finally arrived!

The kitchens had been directed and re-directed to every conceivable location in the vicinity except to the batteries. Len and Al grabbed their mess kits and got in line. The menu was warmed canned salmon ("Goldfish loaf ") and hot coffee. It was their first hot meal in two-and-a-half days. "Oh, Al," Len said. "It's true that hunger is the best sauce."

The next morning the kitchens served cooked bacon, hardtack, and hot coffee. Len and Al felt like royalty dining. It would have been perfect if not for the Germans' habit of lobbing shells to harass their American foes and deny them proper sleep. The Germans were so damned accurate that even the medical wagons weren't spared. Len and Al watched as more than one was blown to smithereens.

The day was largely uneventful, until half past four in the afternoon when German planes appeared overhead. Everyone scurried to find cover before the bombs dropped and machine gun fire from the sky raked the camp. But instead, the German planes dropped propaganda leaflets in the form of mini-American newspapers.

The little newspapers were filled with pictures of fat and happy Dough-boys loving every minute of their time in German captivity. They also contained the names of American POWs, an obvious invitation for the men of the 124th to join their fellow Doughboys on indefinite furlough. The articles were heaped with praise for the Americans, and severe condemnation for their British allies. The question was constantly repeated: why would Americans want to die for Britain, rather than giving up the fight? Len and all the other men raced to scoop up the pamphlets, not for fear of their effect on morale, but for their very practical use in anal hygiene.

The next day wore on everyone's nerves as the Germans kept dropping shells into camp. Yet, Len couldn't help but feel that everyone's guardian angels were especially vigilant—the shells appeared to land anywhere there was an unoccupied piece of ground. It seemed that the troops and most of the equipment were escaping unscathed. The gas klaxons were being banged continuously as the warning cries of "GAS!" echoed throughout the ranks. Masks went on without a hitch as gas clouds blurred the landscape.

Infantry groups were returning from the front for some rest in the rear, following standard procedure by moving at a brisk pace and avoiding the road. It did them no good. The Germans, obviously aware of the movement, lobbed shells on both sides of the road, sending many a Doughboy toward a new destination to meet his maker.

Some of the returning infantry broke ranks and headed for the cover of a nearby cemetery. Len and everyone else tried to wave them off. The artillerymen had surmised from their arrival that the Heinies would already have the graveyard pre-sited, and avoided it like the flu, but the poor infantrymen had no such knowledge and hunkered along the stone walls and grave markers for cover. They quite literally ran into the arms of death as the German shells made short work of them.

Things quieted down considerably as night worn on, but Len was having difficulty sleeping. The whiffing of poison gas combined with the smell of rotting corpses made him wretch, and around 2:00 a.m. he had to leave the pup tent to vomit. The bodies of the infantrymen had been dragged near a ditch and covered. Their boots stuck out from under the horse blanket, and the sight made him sick all over again.

On October 29th, the Germans had four observation balloons over the American artillery positions, giving them a clear view of the entire encampment. Near the balloons, swarming like bees around a hive, were German fighter planes from a Richthofen Jasta, seemingly daring any American planes to make an attempt against the balloons.

The regimental chaplain was racing down the road in broad daylight, heading for the front lines with "goodies" for the boys. Everyone was screaming for him to get off the road but he was oblivious. Len had no use for him. He was not only stupid—the men in the regiment had dubbed him "Charles Chaplain," he was Protestant to boot. The Heinies let loose with a few shells, sending him first into the mud and then running to return to the rear from whence he came. "Good riddance to bad rubbish," Len murmured to himself.

While no one at the time knew it yet, the war would be over in just under two weeks. Len would need that moment of comic relief with the minister, since it would have to last him right through to the armistice. He was about to get back into the thick of the fight, first as an infantryman, then as an artillery scout. He would be involved in some of the nastiest artillery duels of the Great War and death would be his constant companion through it all.

War had made the terrain of the Western Front anything but hospitable;
mobility, especially moving wounded, was a highly difficult task.
Doctors and nurses often had to work in re-enforced holes, amidst
constant shelling and machine gun fire, to treat the wounded. Here,
a Red Cross sign outside an opening denotes the battalion aid station.
—Courtesy of Illinois National Guard

CHAPTER 10

∙∙

In the Death Throes of the Great War

O CTOBER 30TH WAS a fateful day for Battery A of the 124th
Field Artillery. An order from regimental command came down
to the battery commander, the subject—"Accompanying Platoon." The orders read:

1. You will send forward with the infantry at zero hour, D-day, as an
   accompanying platoon, two guns and four caissons with full crews
   and two officers.
2. The officer in command of the platoon will report to P.C. Winn,
   89th Division, before 5 o'clock to-night for further orders.

The day didn't bode well for Len and the rest of the enlisted personnel,
who spent it dodging German shells that landed throughout the camp.
Despite the camouflage netting over the dugouts and casemates, enemy
firing was getting closer and closer to the field guns. If Len had known
that the battery had been given a virtual suicide mission, he probably would
have gone out and stood in the middle of the road.

Military protocol always dictates that in war the artillery moves up
behind the infantry as the infantry advances. If necessitated, it can even
move up with the infantry, but to move up ahead of the infantry could
only be considered insanity. The Allied commanders had demanded, with
an ever-growing intensity, that the artillery advance faster, but this was
carrying things to extremes and now the 124th had become expendable

in a command decision to carry out a desired, but fatally flawed, tactic.

At suppertime, Len and everyone else were still blissfully ignorant of the battery's new orders. The Germans were now dropping mustard shells, so it was masks on for everyone. Fortunately, the kitchen was located atop a hill; since mustard gas always settled in shell holes, foxholes, trenches, and other low lying areas, it was not only desirable but downright healthy to trek up the hill for chow. The musty mask didn't decrease the appetite of Len and the others who had had a lousy breakfast of hardtack fried in bacon grease.

The damn Heinies wouldn't allow a respite even for food. Heavy shells, including 210mms, started raining down. The sense of direction that the battle-tested Doughboys had developed was strong; even though the fogged-over goggles of their gas masks limited their vision, they immediately swung right and headed up the hill.

Along with the heavy caliber shells, the Germans were firing whizz-bangs, which always made those on the receiving end want to shit their pants. Len and Al threw themselves down as their friends on the hillside became casualties. A barracks area took a direct hit, killing everyone inside. Len looked up and saw the cook at the top of the hill running in a panic. This was, of course, the worst thing to do during a barrage. Len started to whisper a prayer for him under his mask, but before he could get out the first few words a screaming piece of shrapnel hit the unfortunate man between the shoulders and he went down.

The situation went from bad to worse as the unmistakable odor of geraniums permeated the air and lightly penetrated everyone's masks—arsenic—the Germans were using arsenic gas! Len motioned to Al and the two men began to crawl down the hill toward the relative safety of the dugouts and their mustard gas clouds. The gas had dissipated enough for them to remove their masks, and they sat down to a dinner of raisins and prunes. Len had a tin of sardines and others had some willy, so the men opened their respective tins and passed them around in a family style fashion.

As they ate, an officer came in and briefed them on the plan for the following two days. There was a collective groan and the officer nodded in agreement. "It's a hell of an assignment, but we don't have any say in the matter. Once we're mobile you artillery scouts will have to reconnoiter the positions for the gun emplacements." The men just hung their heads like scolded children and slowly ate their meal.

On the 31st the engineers and officers who reconnoitered the Bantheville-Landres Road returned near dusk with a plan to try and slip the unit past the Germans in the evening darkness. If it worked, the entire outfit just might make it; if it didn't, they had all just consumed their last meal.

Len had been selected for this mission, but Al had not. Al helped Len ready Annabel as an atmosphere of dread hung over much of the platoon. Al grasped Len's right hand with both of his. "You take care of yourself buddy," he said. "I'll see you when I get up there." Len swallowed hard. "Alright Al," Len said in a near whisper. "Bring some extra rations. The Heinies will probably have a field day blowing our kitchens to hell."

Len put his left foot into the stirrup and threw his right leg over Annabel as he mounted himself in the saddle. Al stroked Annabel's nose. "You take good care of him girl and of yourself too." Len smiled and nodded at Al as he pulled the reins right and moved into formation.

The column moved slowly and quietly forward toward Remonville. There were strict orders that there was to be no talking whatsoever. The column had to move along the edge of enemy occupied woods, through slimy mud valleys past some hills. There was no shortage of American bodies along the roadside.

The quiet gave everyone a chance to think about how dangerous things were and played on everyone's nerves. A caisson took a wrong turn and was lost, and a second one overturned in a shell hole and took 30 minutes to get back into position. A shell landed to the rear and everyone, thinking they were discovered, braced for the worst but nothing more followed.

More bad luck materialized when another caisson got stuck in the mud and took an hour to free. There was shelling up ahead and word of gas attacks from the advanced reconnaissance parties but so far the column had been spared. The inky blackness of the night brought visibility down to near zero, and was especially eerie as it gave the men a sense that danger was stalking them.

A shell burst on a nearby hill sprayed some fragments, but frayed only nerves. The same caisson got stuck yet a third time and everyone cursed as they struggled to get it loose once again. The column continued its advance and passed numerous German bodies. It stopped at the top of a hill, and everyone peered down into a valley that was the front lines. The smell of mustard and arsenic gases along with that of the bloated and rotting corpses made everyone feel that they were about to enter into the bowels of Satan's kingdom.

A squad from the 89th Infantry came up to meet the column. The word was passed in whispered tones that the Germans had listening posts nearby and the smallest noise would bring down a barrage. Len patted Annabel's neck. "It's OK girl," he said reassuringly. "We're going to be fine. Just stay quiet and be a good girl." They started forward and got about halfway through the valley when a chain clanked. That was all it took!

A flare lit up the sky and the Germans started to drop everything they had on the valley. G.I. cans, whizz-bangs, and mustard gas started to fall amongst their ranks. Len whipped on his gas mask and leapt down from Annabel to get her mask on. He finished the task just in time as the valley faded from view amongst the gas clouds. Everyone remained in place trying to hold the animals still as the chaos continued for 30 straight minutes.

An observant officer spotted a small slope and directed the column onto it. The area was clear of gas and the horses were tied to the wagons and fed. Food always proved to be a good distraction for the animals. Everything quieted down as guards were posted and the men assembled in adjoining shell holes. A chain clanked yet again and the Germans once again responded. This time they used the heavier stuff, as 150 and 210mm shells moved along the Bantheville Road. There was nothing to do but stay in the shell holes, hunker down, and pray. The gas masks came on and off as the mustard gas moved in and out of the area with the passing night breeze. It went on that way for two full hours.

Artillery fire or not, it was time to move to higher ground, especially before any rain came and made that impossible by turning the hillside into a pile of goo. Heavy American guns had opened up in the distance and were firing on the Germans' position, but it was not silencing their guns. The officers and NCOs were trying desperately to get the horse teams moving with their artillery pieces, but men and horses alike were dropping like flies. The incessant German fire was wreaking havoc, and the American guns simply could not take it out. The driver of one caisson fell from his saddle and, without hesitation, Sergeant George Ammons, already wounded, jumped up to take his place. He refused any help or medical attention until he had gotten the guns, limber, and horses to a safe position. He was awarded the Distinguished Service Cross for his actions.

Len was wishing he had access to a field buzzer to correct the American counter fire, but there were only engineers for the road and no signal corps people. There was nothing to do but take it and hope for the best. The mustard gas fogged up the area while lenses on the gas masks did the same. The nighttime darkness only added to the column's blindness.

Lieutenant Casey ordered the drivers to wear only the mouthpieces and nose clips from their masks and went to the head of the column to personally lead it up the slope. It was an incredible act of courage on his part and that of the drivers involved. A German shell hit the last caisson in the column and obliterated it entirely—everything from the gun to the horses and drivers. Enemy flares turned the night into day as German machine guns chattered away at the Doughboys and their horses racing past.

If all of this did not fare bad enough, a German 210 mm shell had hit the area along the road, blowing trees out of the ground and onto the column's pathway, creating a natural roadblock. Len was glad he had said good-bye to Al and accepted the fact that he would be in Heaven in no short time.

Depending on one's view, what then came into play was either pure chance or divine intervention. The 90th Infantry Division had machine gunners positioned near enough to spot the flashes from their German counterparts. The 90th raked the German lines with fire as the men from Battery A spotted an opening in the tree line, which they headed toward without delay.

Len glanced back just in time to see the position they had just come from being totally obliterated by the Germans' heavy guns. It was an experience beyond comprehension. The whole incident climaxed with the rising of the morning sun and the counter fire of numerous American batteries against the Germans. A whistle blew and American infantry were charging, bayonets fixed, past Len and the others, on their way to engage the Germans. The column wanted desperately to place their guns and get into the fight but the road and the areas alongside it were strewn with shell holes. Plus, there was little that could be done—47 of the column's 50 engineers had been killed by the shellfire.

It was still far from over as 210mm shells continued to fall. One fell near an American machine gun position and caused it to collapse, but the crew survived and emerged rapidly from the debris. Len's ears were filled with a deafening ring. Annabel was panicking with the others horses, and he was afraid she would throw him. The crossfire between the American and German machine guns was murderous and there was no way to advance through it. One of the officers demonstrated incredible courage as he ran from one American machine gun position to another, exposing himself to fire from both sides, to get them to hold their fire long enough to let the column pass. One of the American crews was atomized as they took a direct hit before the officer could reach them.

With the morning sun, the true extent of the carnage was fully visible. There were dead men and horses everywhere. The platoon and its accompanying engineers had been decimated. There could still be time to place the guns to support the second group of advancing infantry. An officer rode forward with a communication wire that he had gotten riding back under fire, but was killed by an incoming 210 as soon as he handed it over to Lieutenant Casey. His body was placed in a shell hole off to the side of the road.

Len and the column moved along a path through a cluster of trees where wounded American machine gunners lay moaning and dying. Despite their condition, they cheered on the advancing artillerymen. The column emerged just in time to fall in behind the second wave of infantry. The casualty rate among the column had been around fifty percent—five times the "acceptable" military rate.

The Lieutenant ordered the column up the slope. Len dismounted and pulled out his binoculars to examine the enemy lines and assist in placing the guns. He was shocked as he looked over the absolute desolation before him. It looked as if demons had been granted temporary access to the surface of the earth and done their worst. The gas clouds were like drifting snow and obscured his view of the German lines.

Len could see the American infantry advancing and German POWs running forward with their hands in the air. The Doughboys, through sheer force of will and experience with death in great numbers, were driving the Heinies back. French artillery scouts were already on the hill and moving forward. Len could see the enemy lines about three kilometers away and was about to direct the positioning of the guns for the best angle of fire when an American colonel appeared and ordered the column to proceed two kilometers ahead into some woods. "You'll attract fire here!" he yelled repeatedly at Lieutenant Casey, loud enough for everyone to hear.

Len wanted desperately to shoot him. He and the entire column had come through hell to get here. They had lost half their men, a third of the horses, and all but a small handful of the accompanying engineers and now they were being denied the opportunity to fire on the enemy! And why? Because, they might draw fire! What did the stupid bastard think they had drawn during the entire trip along the road?

The entire mission had been for naught. They made it through hell to the outskirts of Remonville just to be told to kiss off. The men cursed like stable boys as they moved off the slope and into the woods. Al and the rest of Battery A caught up with them around suppertime. Al was visibly shaken by what he saw. Other men were crying after seeing the carnage. Len and the others looked like pounded meat. Len glanced up at Al as if he were looking through him and asked almost routinely, "Did you bring those rations? There's no way the kitchens can follow us through this shit!" Al knew Len was experiencing some degree of shock. He nodded slowly in return and pointed toward his saddlebag without saying a word. He dismounted and walked over to his stunned friend.

German shells were still falling in the general vicinity but without effect. "The damn Boche don't realize they're wasting their time and ammo on us," Len said defiantly to Al. "The poor dumb bastards don't know they've already killed most us."

As Len predicted, the kitchens could not possibly come to them. That night the two men dined on Willy and hardtack. Al had managed to secure some manufactured fags (cigarettes) before coming up and they were able to enjoy something other than the customary hand rolled smokes. Len had regained his composure but seemed to want some payback on behalf of the regiment.

Len and Al were up and readying to reconnoiter around 4:00 a.m. on November 2nd. The guns were put in place and ammunition unloaded. Len and Al set out on foot from a grove of trees near Remonville while the rest of the battery set up along further back on the Bantheville Road. The two men had a grid map and binoculars as well as a service buzzer and the wire an officer had given his life for.

The German lines were just over a kilometer away, and the men plotted the coordinates on the map and relayed them back to the platoon echelon in the grove to their rear. They watched in eager anticipation as a barrage opened on the enemy position. They called back some correction in fire only to be informed that nothing more was to be fired. There were simply too few shells that had made it to the forward area. The Germans probably figured it was only intended as harassing fire and didn't respond.

Len and Al remained in position and were contacted by phone around 9:30 that morning. The Germans had made no major altercations in their position, though their guns remained camouflaged, and since they had failed to return fire earlier, there were no muzzle flashes to observe and thus no gun positions to report. The barrage conducted by the battery at 10:00 a.m. was pathetic. It was even lighter than the one four-and-a-half hours earlier. The Germans hardly seemed to take notice. The two scouts were informed that the battery was out of ammunition.

Len and Al were ordered to return to the platoon. When they returned they found that more ammunition had been brought up, and it smelled like some small cooking fires were about to brew coffee. Len needed it. There was a cold and continuous mist spraying. This, combined with little sleep, no hot chow, and a tremendous degree of stress, was making him sick.

Len was developing a dry cough. He was worried, as he had been weeks earlier when stricken with severe diarrhea. Then, he had been required to examine his stools for blood, which would have meant dysentery. Now, he would have to watch for sputum and see if there was any blood in that. That would mean pneumonia, or possibly influenza, and that would mean almost certain death.

Len was sleeping deeply when he and Al were awakened at 2:00 a.m. on the morning of November 3rd. The orders were for the battery to move forward. It was raining, a cold and unwelcoming night. Within 30 minutes, they were on the move. The Germans were falling back and the infantry and artillery were to dog them all the way.

It was encouraging that by noon the platoon was replenished with men and ammo, and while no hot food was available, there was a plentiful supply of field rations. This combined with word that the German aerodrome at Barricourt had been abandoned did much to lift morale. Even the German artillery fire was far off the mark, falling well to the column's rear. It was obvious to Len and Al that the Germans were not using scouts, but the coordinates from the battery's last known position. The Heinies were on the run.

The infantry continued to move up in single file ranks while some trucks with women in German uniforms came from the opposite direction. Were these prostitutes or were the Huns putting women, as well as children, into uniform? Lieutenant Casey spotted the corpse of a topless woman laying on the edge of a machine gun pit. Having no need for artillery scouts at the moment, he ordered Len and Al to wrap her in a horse blanket and bury her.

After finishing the job, the two men mounted up and rode back toward the front of the column, where they learned that their assigned destination was Barricourt. They reached Remonville, where the Germans had made an orderly and hard-fought retreat. There was some enemy shellfire falling, but it didn't require any expertise to time it. The Heinies were firing a barrage, five minutes long, every quarter hour. All the Americans had to do was to wait for it to lift and then make good on the ten minutes of quiet.

Messengers brought word that Barricourt was now in American hands and that the infantry was fighting near Tailly. The Germans were being pushed back to the Meuse River. The infantry had rolling kitchens at Remonville but there was no way to make use of them, as they too were moving. In fact, everyone and everything was moving, or at least trying to move, but the incline of the ground leading out of Remonville was so muddy, steep, and filled with shell holes that it was rapidly becoming a supreme cluster fuck.) *a favorite phrase*

Some infantrymen showed some real initiative and overturned a kitchen into a deep ditch. It worked beautifully as a bridge. Len dismounted and led Annabel across by her reins. Things were moving in an orderly single file fashion, but there was no longer any telling who belonged to what unit. Artillerymen were mixed with infantry, infantry with cooks and their kitchens, kitchens with ambulances and so on. It was still a cluster fuck, but at least it was an organized cluster fuck. *awful.*

At the top of the hill the battery pulled out of the advancing column to care for the horses. The hill was strewn with the remains of a couple dozen German corpses and their horses. They were the remnants of some German 77mm field guns that the American artillery had "neutralized." After what Len had experienced on the road two nights ago, it was hard to have much sympathy. Still, he made a silent request for God to have mercy on their souls.

The column continued toward Barricourt and reached the outskirts at daybreak. They were ordered to place their horses and equipment off the road in the woods just outside of town. There was a house still standing. Len pointed to it and said to Al, "Let's go in there and get dry and see if we can't find a corner to crib out in." The two men joined the long line of artillerymen entering as well, only to find that this was no place to stay. Every bed and square foot of space was already occupied. The men had entered a makeshift morgue and the only prone Doughboys were corpses. There was a collective gasp as the men jammed the doorway pushing and shoving to get out.

November 4th was spent in eager anticipation as word went back and forth as to whether the battery would move up to Beauclair or Laneuville. The word came down at 3:30 p.m. that it was the latter. A barrage was put on Laneuville, while infantry advanced just behind it. Len and Al directed fire on the town until they were ordered to stop to allow the infantry to move in. It was somewhat satisfying to be on the delivering end of the artillery for a change.

The following day was overcast, and Len and Al were ordered to ride ahead to scout enemy positions. The village of Stenay was now under assault, and the fleeing civilians were clogging the roads and surrounding area. The scouts would have to pinpoint the enemy positions around Laneuville and toward Stenay to avoid friendly fire on Doughboys and civilians alike. The mission saved their lives. Shortly after the two men rode off, two German shells landed in the firing position of Battery A, killing most of the cannoneers. Len and Al had been having breakfast and drinking coffee with these men just a short time earlier.

The two scouts returned at suppertime with the necessary coordinates of the enemy's positions, and it was then that they learned that many of their comrades from the battery were dead. But there was no time to mourn, as the entire regiment was being ordered forward. The field guns needed to be moved to the heights above Laneuville so they could fire on the high ground along the Meuse River.

When the regiment reached the heights overlooking Laneuville they were ordered not to place the guns but to move through the town using the Beaumont Road. Len and everyone else knew this would subject them to the same type of butchering they had endured along the Bantheville-Landres Road a few days earlier. The Germans were burning their own supplies, including signal flares, during their rapid retreat, and that night the skies along the Meuse River glowed an eerie red and green.

The regiment got through Laneuville with minimal German harassment. They then spent the night camped out and exposed on the wet, cold ground around Beauclair. It had rained and the blankets were soaked through. Al nudged Len awake, because Len was shivering so badly that his teeth were chattering. He had a fever and was badly chilled. "Oh Dear God," Len moaned. "What I wouldn't give for some cognac." That was the only medicine and it was damn hard to come by. "I'll get some hot coffee Len," Al said reassuringly. "I'll see what I can do about the cognac."

Some of the men who were ill were getting strychnine injections. It was believed by physicians at the time to be a useful "tonic" in small doses. Len had no medical training but he rightfully regarded most of the injections of the day as pure quackery and was not about to report for sick call. He'd get cognac and raw eggs or die in his saddle, but he'd be damned before he'd let the medical corps experiment on him.

Len saddled up with Al riding close alongside to catch him if he started to slip from the saddle. The guns were placed near the Meuse River, and the scouts planted themselves there for a late lunch. Gun cotton was readily available so Al heated up their cans of Willy, reasoning that a hot meal was more soothing for Len than a cold one. The two men used their binoculars to observe the mad rush of civilians clogging the roads out of Stenay and all the surrounding villages.

The men had to conduct themselves carefully, as German snipers were on the other side of the river. No doubt American ones were busy too, taking shots at any Germans exposing themselves during their retreat. Word came from Laneuville that the church steeple had been taken out by German artillery. There was no one in it. It was too obvious a target and no longer needed for observation.

On November 7th Len and Al were still overlooking the Meuse River, watching the German retreat and verifying the deflection and range as the batteries dropped shells where they could be relatively certain of avoiding civilians. Replacements were coming up, but they were in their late teens and had been put in uniform and shipped to Europe less than two weeks prior. Other than knowing how to salute and march, they had no training whatsoever. "Damn it to hell," Len said. "We're as bad as the Heinies! What the hell are we going to do with these kids?" It was decided to get them toward the rear supply wagons and keep them away not only from the frontline but also from the fuses and shells altogether.

When Len's health couldn't seem to get any worse, a corporal came up with a small bundle. "Fairfield!" he called out. "Get over here." Len pulled himself up to a wobbling standing position and forced himself over. "I know you and some of the others are ailing," he said. "Be discreet and see that this gets around." Len glanced inside to see it was cognac and real eggs. "Thank you corporal," he gasped. "Thank you very much!" The corporal nodded then turned around and left. Len clued in Al who promptly went to round up their ill buddies. Cognac and raw eggs were administered to the close-knit group. There was even a little cognac left over which was to be kept for Len by unanimous consent.

Because of their position along the heights of the Meuse, Len and Al could assist the firing batteries without leaving the guns. As the American fire increased, the German fire continued to lessen. It was obvious the Germans were beaten. It was now just a matter of when they'd admit it to themselves.

On November 9th the infantry began to assemble in force in the surrounding woods. The word was that they would cross the Meuse near

Pouilly at any time. The 11th Field Artillery had moved their guns up with the 124th, and the rain of fire falling on the Germans was impressive. Len and Al were spotting muzzle flashes from German artillery, which was firing sporadically and without any real effect. It was obvious they were shooting blind.

On November 10th the 122nd relieved the 124th, who were sent back to Laneuville for some rest and hot chow. They'd need it. Word was that the infantry would cross the Meuse the flowing day and the 124th would be sent into Pouilly to take up position after the village had been secured.

Al helped Len into an area near a rolling kitchen. There was hot soup and Len still had a little cognac left. The engineers, supply wagons, ammunition trains, ambulances, boats and infantry were all moving forward toward the Meuse for the following day's action. It was a regular Big Parade.

Around 2:00 a.m. on November 11th, Len and Al were awakened by a near-deafening barrage falling on the German positions on the other side of the Meuse. The Infantry was crossing the river with only scattered resistance, and the Germans were on the run. Enemy artillery was shelling the roadway but by now it was too late. Everything needed was already at the river and in the process of crossing over.

Len was too sick to care and too experienced to be bothered by the cannon fire. It was for him more a matter of going unconscious than simply falling asleep. He awoke around 6:00 a.m. by Al shaking him. Len looked up with dismay, "Why did you do that Al? I was sound asleep and could have stayed that way for another hour," he said with a horribly raspy voice.

Al was grinning from ear to ear, which puzzled Len all the more. "Len, command got word about a half hour ago." Len propped himself up on one elbow as he tried to wipe the sleep out of his eyes with his other hand. "Word about what?" Are we moving into Pouilly?"

"No," Al said enthusiastically. "The Germans want an armistice. It all ends today at 11:00 o'clock this morning! It all ends today Len, today!" Len sat up and pointed toward a coffee pot. "Today you get breakfast in bed or at least on the ground," Al chirped. There was even something hot to eat—hardtack fried in bacon grease.

"How do we know this is real?" Len asked. "We've heard this kind of bunk before." One of the NCOs leaned downwards. "It's real Fairfield.

The officers have been spreading word for about the better part of an hour." As if to call him a liar, a German 77mm shell landed in the road spraying earth chunks all over them. It was responded to in kind by the 155mm big guns of the 11th Field Artillery. "Over, huh?" grunted Len.

Then runners came from the command post and the telephone dugout that official word had come from Pershing, as well as radio communications from Paris. The Germans had signed an armistice and all hostilities were to cease at 11:00 a.m. on the dot. That seemed certain enough for everyone concerned. All everyone had to was stay quiet and low for the next two-and-a-half hours and everything would be just jake.

There was about a thirty-minute reprieve until the German guns opened up around 9:00 o'clock. "What the hell is this?" Len asked with incredulity. "It's all about to end. Why should anybody die now?" The shells were falling harmlessly in the road but American guns were responding. Then about fifteen minutes later the officers said that the rate of return fire was to be reduced and stopped altogether by 10:00 o'clock.

Unfortunately, the Germans weren't going to go out quietly. A shell landed on the American camp and killed seven men. Curses and demands for retribution rose in chorus amongst the Doughboys. Another German shell landed directly on a sawmill and killed God knows how many. Then with a little over twenty minutes to go, a Heinie shell hit the kitchen area of the 11th Field Artillery and killed over a dozen.

That was the last straw! Orders or no orders, the cannoneers from the 11th ran to their 155s and opened up with everything they had on the German positions across the river. "It's about time," said Al. "I'd even spot for them if they needed it," Len replied. The officers from the 11th were running amongst the gun crews waving their arms and yelling for the men to cease firing, but the crews continued unabated.

With the Great War to end at 11:00 o'clock on the 11th day of the 11th month, someone must have reasoned that it was only fitting that the 11th Field Artillery fire the final round. The crews knew the fateful moment was growing near, and finally deferred to their officers and slowed their rate of fire as the final seconds ticked away. An officer pointed at "Calamity Jane," a 155mm gun and the favorite of the unit.

The officer carefully followed the second hand as it moved around the face of his watch. Finally, at the last second of 10:59 a.m. he thrust his hand downwards and the final round of the war was fired. Smoke was rising from the guns and the camouflage paint on the barrels bubbled. There was no more firing by either side. It was over. A few men cheered while others sang, "It's over, over here."

"We made it Len, we made it!" Al yelled as he slapped his friend heartily on the back. Len didn't look so good. His cough sounded somewhat raspy. "Are you OK Len?" Al asked. Len simply turned his pale face toward his friend. "Al," he said. "I've never felt better in my life."

Len's unit ordered to keep up w/ infantry to Renanville

Doughboys in LaRochette, Luxembourg take a break from post war occupation duties to enjoy a cup of hot chocolate courtesy of the American YMCA. Notice the Yellow Cross insignia of the 33rd Infantry Division on the upper sleeves of the soldiers' uniforms.—Courtesy of the Illinois National Guard

CHAPTER 11

Occupation, Recuperation, and Demobilization

THE WAR'S END BROUGHT an immediate improvement in Len's physical condition. It was as if a huge weight, in the form of a large haversack, had been lifted from his shoulders. That night there was celebrating aplenty as flares, illumination shells, and smoke created a festival-like atmosphere. Somehow there was no longer a shortage of cognac and there were plenty of inebriated Doughboys.

The celebrations went on up and down the American side of the Meuse. It seemed to be done in such a way as to stick a finger in the eye of the defeated enemy. General Pershing had given strict orders against any fraternization with the Germans, and those orders were being rigidly adhered to by the 58th despite the best efforts of their former foes to communicate and socialize. It was still just an armistice and there was always the remote possibility that hostilities could resume.

Stenay was to become the new home for the 58th FAB for the next two months. Life there resembled what things had been like in early September. Supplies continued to arrive and had to be stockpiled. There was continuous drilling and training. The equipment and animals were put into the best possible shape while the men enjoyed a marked improvement in the quality of hot food now served at normal intervals.

The Red Cross was established in force and the heavenly aroma of fresh hot donuts once again filled the air. Len had written Maggie on the day of the armistice to let her know that he was alive and "well." A bundle of letters from her had accumulated, since Len's unit had been almost inaccessible due to the heavy enemy bombardment it had sustained during the last eleven days of the war.

Christmas of 1918 was a joyful event, even if tempered by homesickness. The French civilians in the area did all they could to make their American Allies feel welcome and, despite shortages in materials, baked cookies and small cakes. Len got a scarf in the mail from Maggie, and he sent her a brooch.

There was snow, and kids appeared, wanting the brave "soldats" to share their sleds in a ride with them down a local rise. Len and Al gladly obliged and took turns zooming downward at near breakneck speed on sleds far too overcrowded with kids, who held on tightly and laughed hysterically the whole way down. The soldiers laughed just as hard and most tumbled over when they reached the bottom.

Orders came down after the New Year for the brigade to leave Stenay and march into Luxembourg where it would serve as part of the Army of Occupation in Reserve. The unit moved out on January 4th with more mules than horses pulling wagons and guns. The horses had fared no better than their human counterparts in battle, but like Len, Annabel had been a miraculous survivor. The march took five days, and the brigade's headquarters was established in Schoenfels just south of Diekirch. The 124th was billeted nearby in Berschbach and would remain there until being ordered home.

The Germans occupied Luxembourg almost immediately after the outbreak of war in 1914 and the populace had no use for the Boche. The Germans had been hard occupiers and sucked the small nation nearly dry of its resources. The timely arrival of American troops from the 58th FAB had prevented the retreating Germans from any additional pillaging, and the local populace was so thrilled that they celebrated with a festival complete with dancing and alcohol to honor their liberators. This history would repeat itself in September of 1944 and again in early 1945.

On the following day, January 10th, the infantry of the 33rd Division was re-united with its artillery units and the 58th Field Artillery Brigade ceased to be an independent organization. To mark the occasion, there was an evening of celebration, food, and festivities at the Hotel de l'Europe, a famed summer resort in Diekirch.

Duties were sparse. For Len, they consisted mostly of the care of Annabel and an occasional sentry posting. Len now had the time and inclination to paint the Divisional insignia on the front of his helmet. Life was simply a matter of marking the days until the return trip home.

Len participated in a horse show conducted in the Diekirch town square on February 27th, attended by no less than the Grand Duchess of Luxembourg. It was, however, rainy and quite cold, and Len absorbed plenty of both. The next day he awoke feeling feverish and very ill. He reported for sick call.

He was admitted to the hospital with a diagnosis of pneumonia/influenza. There was acetylsalicylic acid (aspirin) to help with the fever and muscle aches but, as he had always feared, most of what was done was quackery. He was given injections of strychnine that did nothing other than make him vomit and suffer near dehydration.

On March 19th, doctors re-administered the "vaccines" for typhoid and paratyphoid that he had originally received during his basic training at Camp Logan. It was an act of desperation on the part of physicians, who hoped that the administration of any vaccine whatsoever would stimulate the immune system and give the patient a better chance of combating any disease(s) that afflicted them. It was pseudo-science and provided no clinical benefit, while frequently doing great harm. The paratyphoid vaccine was dubious at best and even if it had been effective against typhoid, it would do nothing against either flu or pneumonia.

Len continued to lose weight and get sicker. He was beginning to accept the idea that he would not recover, though he decided against letting Maggie know. Why have her worry? It certainly wouldn't do any good, and she would have plenty of time to mourn after she got official word of his death.

The administration of blackberry wine did calm Len's intestines and he began to slowly regain control over his bowels. This enabled him to retain a diet rich in chicken soup, cheese, cooked vegetables, and apples, all of which seemed to help. By the end of March he was released from the hospital, though walking on very wobbly legs. He missed the regimental band concert at Rollingen on St. Patrick's Day, as well as the big horse competition in Luxembourg City (the nation's capital) in which the 33rd Division took high honors, beating out both the 5th and 7th Infantry Divisions.

Because of his five-week illness, Len also missed out on the Class "C" passes for a three-day leave to Paris. They could keep it, as far as he was concerned. All he wanted to do was go home, and as it turned out, he wouldn't have long to wait. Official word arrived at the division on April 15th that they were to leave for Brest, and the big boat home, on April 24th.

On April 22nd the division was in Ettelbruck, Luxembourg, where it stood for inspection by no less than AEF Commander and General of the Army, John J. Pershing. Also present were Secretary of War Newton Baker, Prince Leopold of Belgium, and British Major General Keppel-Bethel. Len was still weak but stood in formation and knew the outfit looked damn fine. The following day the division received Field Order #39, which stated they were to be ready to board trains bound for Brest, and then home. The 124th never got trains in Luxembourg and simply marched out of the country on April 28th. Len was among those privileged to ride their mounts. On May 7th there was a ceremony in France for the 33rd's commander, Major General George Bell, Jr., where he received the French Legion of Honor, France's highest military decoration.

There was also the requirement to turn in mounts. Len was never an overly sentimental guy, especially when it came to animals, but Annabel had been something different. They had survived a great deal together and had developed a real bond between them. Before parting Len cut some apples into slices and sprinkled them liberally with sugar.

It was as if Annabel suspected their imminent parting and seemed to keep her eyes fixed on Len as she gobbled the treats he fed her. "I'll miss you ole girl," he whispered in her ear so that no one else could hear. "We've been through a lot together, and I really wish I could take you with me. Now you take good care of yourself." He ran his hand down her face one last time. Then he handed the reins to the remount NCO, turned and walked away, haunted by the feeling that he was leaving an old friend.

The infantry regiments of the 33rd Division sailed on May 7th and landed in New York on the 17th, where they were met by Illinois Governor Frank Lowden. Once again, the artillery was not so fortunate. Len, Al, and the others from the 124th boarded the *America* on May 16th, which sailed that same day for Hoboken, New Jersey. The trip home was on relatively calm seas, with no zigzagging necessary to avoid enemy submarines, but Len still had no trouble "feeding the fish" several times on the journey home. The ship docked in Hoboken on the 24th.

The men of the 124th, like most of the 33rd Division, were sent to Camp Mills on Long Island for the initial stage of reprocessing. Len and his comrades had signed and addressed standardized cards while on the *America*, stating that they had arrived back in the states alive and well. These cards were mailed to relatives as soon as the ship docked in Hoboken.

While at Camp Mills, the men of the 33rd Division learned that they were going to return to Chicago by train, with their arrival scheduled for the morning of Wednesday, June 5th. Some 13 trains, arriving at four different stations, would each be met by a welcoming reception of relatives scheduled for 9:30 a.m. Len was concerned about how Maggie might react to his gaunt appearance—he didn't want her to try navigating such a sea of humanity, so he didn't bother to inform her of this event. Instead, he wrote and informed her that he would be discharged on June 8th at Camp Grant (Rockford). He would take the train back to Chicago and meet her that afternoon at his parents' house. He did, however, let her know that he had been ill, and though he was now recovered, he had "lost weight."

The homecoming parade in Chicago started at 11:00 a.m., led by none other than the regiment's original commander, Colonel Horatio Hackett. The War Department, for some unknown reason, would not authorize the entire division to pass in review, so the artillery units re-formed their old brigade and marched from the train depot to Grant Park, as General Bell and Governor Lowden watched from the reviewing stand in front of the Art Institute on Michigan Avenue.

Refreshments were served to the returning troops during ninety-minute receptions at several posh hotels in the Loop. These included the Hotels Morrison, Sherman, and LaSalle as well as the Blackstone, Congress, Auditorium, and Stratford. The troops then boarded trains at 3:00 p.m. to take them back to what had been their point of origin 18 months earlier—Camp Grant in Rockford.

There were a few days for packing and processing before the 124th

Field Artillery was demobilized and its members honorably discharged on Saturday, June 8, 1919.

First Lieutenant Donald Stier, commanding Battery A, completed the blank sections on Len's Form 525 (Honorable Discharge) in well-formed cursive. Len received back pay of $83.58 along with a $60.00 bonus. The document rated both his horsemanship and physical condition as "Good" at the time of discharge and listed his personal character as "Excellent." Under the remarks section he wrote that Len had no AWOLs, proving that his night with Maggie while he was stationed at Camp Merritt had clearly been overlooked. Lieutenant Stier signed the document and then slid it across the table for Len to do the same. After he did, the Lieutenant extended his hand and congratulated him on a job well done. In fact, it was a job well done by the entire regiment.

The 58th Field Artillery Brigade had 55 men killed in action or dead from wounds or disease. With 39 of these belonging to the 124th, the regiment, by far, had the highest number of losses in the Brigade. The 124th lost 18 privates, 5 first class privates, 1 wagoner, 3 mechanics, 5 corporals, 3 sergeants, 2 second lieutenants, a first lieutenant, and a captain. There were nine men (one posthumously) who were awarded the Distinguished Service Cross. The decoration is second only to the Medal of Honor.

Lt. Col. Joseph Rogers was cited by General Pershing for Meritorious and Conspicuous Service. There were 140 additional officers and enlisted men who received citations for Gallantry from either General Bell or General Pershing and a further 17 who were cited for Gallantry by both generals.

General Charles P. Summerall, commanding general of the First Infantry Division in September and October of 1918, commended the 58th FAB for the Brigade's support during the fighting at St. Mihiel. Summerall's chief of staff wrote the following on September 14, 1918 to the 58th FAB (Gen. Todd commanding) in regards to St. Mihiel:

The Division Commander (Summerall) desires me to express to you and all of the officers and men of the 58th Field Artillery Brigade his commendation of your gallant conduct in the recent operations against the St. Mihiel salient. The loyalty and devotion exhibited in moving forward your batteries over the most difficult country under the worst weather conditions are worthy of the best traditions of the field artillery. The skill and efficiency with which the guns were served are evidences of the high standards that obtains in the Brigade.

This was soon followed by General Edwin Winans, commander of the 64th Infantry Brigade, who sent a letter of appreciation to General Todd on October 10th stating that the 58th's supporting fire during the capture of Bois de la Morine, Bois du Chene Sec, and Gesnes was "prompt and accurate" and that there was, "not a single report of friendly shots during this operation."

Promoted to command V Corps in October 1918, General Summerall sent a letter of commendation on November 2nd to General D.E. Altman, commander of V Corps Artillery (including the 58th FAB) for their supporting fire along the Meuse during the intense fighting there on November 1st. The motto eventually bestowed upon the 124th Field Artillery was one well deserved: *Facta Non Verba*—Deeds, Not Words.

As a whole, the 33rd Infantry Division had an exemplary record. There were 8 men awarded the Medal of Honor and 110 received the Distinguished Service Cross. From Britain, one man was awarded the Distinguished Service Order, 5 the Military Cross, 5 the Distinguished Conduct Medal and 41 the Military Medal. France awarded 47 men the Croix de Guerre, and Belgium awarded one man the Order of Leopold (Officer Grade). From the time it left Camp Logan, through to the Armistice, there were only two officers tried by General Court Martial and no enlisted personnel whatsoever.

In regards to his division, General Bell wrote the following from Camp Grant in November of 1919:

The 33rd Division accomplished every task assigned to it. Not a single failure is recorded against it. Not a single scandal occurred to mar the glory of its achievements.

Duty to God, to country and to home, well done, is the highest standard humanly attainable. The officers and men of the 33rd

Division did their duty superbly. Their deeds and the example which they set are imperishable. Illinois may well be proud of her sons, both the living and the dead.

Len and Al were content being amongst the vast numbers devoid of recognition for individual gallantry, but still more than satisfied with their service. They had honorably done their duty in war and lived, and by doing so, they knew war's only glory and victory—survival. They boarded the "Q" for the ride back to Chicago. They talked and, on occasion, even laughed of their experiences and their eagerness to return to family and civilian life. They exchanged addresses and would remain close friends all their lives.

The red chevron on the sleeve of each man designated their Honorable Discharge and allowed them to ride the rails for free. They also had two gold chevrons (homemade as the army did not issue official versions until the 1920s) on their sleeve with each one designating 6 months of overseas service.

In 1919 Congress would authorize the Great War Victory Medal. Len and Al would be eligible for the medal with three metal "Battle Clasps." One to denote service for action at "St. Mihiel," a second for the "Meuse-Argonne" Offensive, and a third for the "Defensive Sector," which denoted small actions not part of a full campaign. They were also eligible to wear the Victory Lapel Pin in Bronze (Silver for those wounded in action). The Occupation Medal was only awarded to those whose occupation duty was performed in Germany proper or Austria-Hungary.

Some 85 years later, Len's Grandson would obtain the appropriate, yet unofficial, commemorative campaign medals awarded by various French cities and veterans' organizations. These included the Medal of Verdun (award #197-126), the Liberation Medal of St. Mihiel (issued in 1936), and the Argonne-Vauquois Medal (issued in 1961 to WWI vets still living at the time).

Maggie was waiting with her in-laws when Len arrived that fateful Saturday afternoon. He was home. He was really home! She wanted to leap into his arms, but it was obvious from his rather frail appearance that he was still underweight from his bout with pneumonia and flu, as well as his frequent exposure to poison gas and battlefield living. She settled for a hug and kiss. Len had understated his condition so as not to worry her.

Now that they were together again everything seemed possible. They had no way of knowing at the time the hardships that lay before them: the Great Depression of the 1930s, a larger and longer world conflict that would greatly affect their children, and a relegation by history to what would become known as the "Lost Generation." Still, while there is life, there is hope, and that is what occupied their thoughts, as they were ready to brave all challenges and begin a new life together.

1918 photo of Maggie as "Liberty Lady," from a war rally.

Epilogue

L EN RETURNED TO CIVILIAN life with jubilation. He and Maggie rented a small apartment for $30 a month and furnished it with second-hand pieces. Len also returned to his old job as a valveman at the gas works.

Domestic life for the newlyweds had its ups and downs. For example, Maggie had a lot to learn about cooking. One Friday she made fresh fish for dinner. The only problem was that she unaware it had to be scaled before it was breaded, cooked, and eaten. Len took one bite and promptly emptied the plate out the window.

The budget was tight, but life had plenty of light moments. Once, Len needed a new belt. The belt cost ten cents and that happened to be exactly the same price for two tickets to the flickers. The decision was that the belt could wait but the flickers couldn't.

Len's best man was now an up-and-coming young executive with Union Carbide. Len knew he had no future at the gas works and wrote his friend inquiring about his help in finding a better job. The answer was swift. A chief clerk was needed at their Prest-O-Lite (part of Linde Air Products) Plant in Hammond, Indiana. He was told to learn everything he could about acetylene. Len did and he got the job.

Len was soon promoted to assistant superintendent. One day he filled in for the superintendent, who had become ill, but the superintendent never returned and soon Len was running the entire operation. It was a time when self-taught men who worked hard could rise to prominent positions in business, without the benefit of extensive formal education.

A heavy smoker himself, Len was always a bug about safety, yet there was never a serious accident during his entire time as superintendent—an amazing record for a man who was responsible for a plant that refilled and painted tanks containing highly combustible gases of varying types.

Still, there was some excitement. One evening in the 1920s, when Len was alone at the plant doing paperwork, a few of Al Capone's people showed up looking to hide some ladies of ill repute from lawmen who were raiding their local brothel. While not approving of prostitution, Len was never sympathetic to the coppers of the day who seldom seemed to give the little guy a break, and besides it didn't seem a wise move to refuse Capone people in need. He hid the girls in the plant for an hour or so until the gangsters returned to pick them up. When they drove off, they threw a large wad of bills on the platform in gratitude. It was "blood money," which couldn't be kept, so Len and Maggie dropped the entire stash into the church poor box.

There was also a year of unexpected bachelorhood for Len, when Maggie brought the children to the "ole sod" of Ireland for a family visit in 1924. While there, she required emergency surgery for an acute bout of hyperthyroidism. She came within an eyelash of dying on the operating table, and her recovery was a slow and painful process.

Maggie and Len were prolific. They had ten children, including Mary (1920–2004), whose husband, Mike Bilder, served as a rifleman in WWII and fought in some of the same areas of France as Len. He was also in Diekirch, where he fought during the Battle of the Bulge. Mike was one of the few people Len would ever discuss his combat experiences with.

Then came Leonard (1921–2005), who became a Carmelite Priest and took the religious name of Jeffry when ordained in 1946. Father Jeffry served in many places, including nine years in Lima, Peru, and as a chaplain at a VA Hospital in Bath, New York. When vets on their deathbed expressed their fear of dying to Father Jeffry, he would simply say, "I'll hold one hand and God will hold the other and together we'll take you across." He died in a retirement center for Carmelites in Los Angeles.

Bill was third (1924–1971). He earned a degree in journalism from Northwestern and went on to have a successful career in advertising and public relations. He was a first lieutenant in the 10th Mountain Division and arrived in Italy just in time—for VE Day! He was called back to army service during the Korean conflict but was fortunate enough to be assigned to the Public Information Office (PIO). He and his wife Jean had three boys and lived in Willoughby, a suburb of Cleveland. A heavy smoker, he died at 47 from lung cancer.

Dorothea was next (1926–2010). She was trained in nursing at Little Company of Mary Hospital and earned her RN there. She married John Mumm, a navigator on B-24s, who served in Europe. John earned a Masters Degree in Nuclear Engineering and even worked on a part of the Nautilus, America's first nuclear powered submarine. Together, they raised five children.

Joe (1927–1989) was number five. A college graduate, he served stateside in the army during the Korean conflict. He never married but was a partner in his own real estate agency (Post Realty) in Evergreen Park, a Chicago suburb. Like his father and brother Bill, he too was a heavy smoker. He developed oral cancer in 1982 and suffered with treatments until his death seven years later.

Gerard was born in 1928. A lifelong bachelor, he entered the Army Air Corps after high school and served as a control tower operator at Muroc (Edwards) Air Base. He obtained a law degree from Kent and went on to become a Vice-President at the First National Bank of Chicago (now Chase), retiring in 1986.

Therese (1929–2006) was number seven. Like her sister Dorothea, she became a nurse. In 1952 she married Claude Akins who became a renowned character actor in movies and on TV. During the 1970s he starred in his own TV series, "The Misadventures of Sheriff Lobo." They raised three children and enjoyed long lives together. Claude passed away in 1994.

Margaret was born in 1932 and like her sisters, Dorothea and Therese, became a nurse. She studied for three years at St. Francis Hospital in Evanston, IL. Years later, she went on to obtain a bachelor's degree in nursing and a graduate degree in counseling psychology. She specialized in counseling trauma victims, including those involved in the 1989 San Francisco earthquake. She and her husband raised four children.

Gene was born in 1933. After college, he served with the 3rd Infantry Division (1954–56) in the Public Information Office (PIO). He and his wife, Grace, raised six children. Gene and his family relocated to the east coast for his work with IBM, where he eventually became a Director in the company's Communications Department before retiring.

Ann, born in 1937, was the tail ender. She and her husband Chuck, an engineer, raised three children and still live on the West coast. She had a career in education until retirement.

Len helped those in need of a job whenever he could. He even hired his own father. Len was there at his dad's deathbed when he died from colon cancer in 1935 at Little Company of Mary Hospital.

Len and Maggie enjoyed the economic prosperity of the 1920s, and he was happy in fatherhood. Len often carried Mary on his shoulders up to bed, singing the World War I song, "Just a Baby's Prayer at Twilight." But his all-time favorite song from the Great War was, like Dwight Eisenhower, "Roses of Picardy." Still, the war largely faded from his conscious thoughts; his helmet became just a flowerpot on the outside porch.

He once took young Mary to the racetrack and let her pick a horse to bet on. She picked the horse with the lightest jockey because she figured it could run the fastest. Len plunked down a $2.00 bet and the long shot horse won. He bought Mary a new dress on the way home. In 1933 he took her to the Chicago World's Fair but avoided the infamous and highly popular burlesque dancer Sally Rand, as he was every inch a gentleman. He even wore a necktie to go to the grocery store.

There was a family cottage on Flint Lake, near Valparaiso, which was a favorite family getaway. In 1930, the depression hit like a bombshell, and Len, reared in poverty and forever terrified of it, worried greatly throughout the decade about his job and supporting his family. The decade wore on him considerably and depressed his demeanor at home. The fact that Len was paid only once a month made the family budget all that much tighter.

Al Slowey, who never married, was a regular Friday night visitor and the two men enjoyed a liberal consumption of beer during his visits. When Al's employer, the Chicago and Alton Railroad, faded out of existence, Len got him a job. On Friday nights the two men often conceived of Rube Goldberg projects that included hooking the hot water heater up to the toilet to prevent the bowl water from freezing one winter. Len nearly scalded his rear when using the jerry-rigged contraption for the first time.

Remembering his alcoholic father, Len never drank on work nights or cashed a paycheck. His job worries during the 1930s were unfounded. Union Carbide thought highly of him and even offered him a promotion to their home office in West Virginia. He turned it down, fearing there were too few Catholics there for his children to meet and marry.

World War II brought a return to economic prosperity but, as a combat veteran, Len knew all too well of the suffering of young American boys. He had to register for the draft in 1943, but since he was already fifty and a veteran of the previous world war there was no worry of his being called up. He loved the German war ballad "Lilli Marlene" which was popular on both sides of the lines.

Allied victory in 1945 pushed away the dark clouds that had hovered over Len for the previous fifteen years, and produced a marked improvement in his mood and outlook. He did, however, always hold fast to his belief that American involvement in the First World War was a mistake. In his mind, America's entry into the conflict did more harm than good. He maintained that the Europeans would have been forced to come to terms acceptable to all parties if the United States had remained neutral.

In regards to World War II, he shared the view of his son-in-law Mike, that the Russians should never have been allowed to stay in Eastern Europe after Germany's defeat. "All we did was take the "P" out of Prussia," he often said.

The Great War left one profound sense of trauma that remained with Len all his life—he forever wretched at the smell of spoiled meat. Something as seemingly innocuous as cold cuts having gone south in the icebox could trigger this reaction.

Len stayed with Prest-O-Lite from 1919 until his retirement almost forty years later. Upon retirement he and Maggie moved out to the "country"—the tiny Village of Worth, a suburb southwest of Chicago that was at the time a very sparsely populated rural community. Their grandson would serve two terms as mayor there during the 1990s.

Len had been a strong supporter of Al Smith in 1928, but opposed Kennedy's election in 1960 despite his Catholic faith. Len regarded Kennedy as too young and inexperienced, and felt that the Bay of Pigs fiasco, Kennedy's poor performance at the Vienna Summit with Khrushchev, and the construction of the Berlin Wall, all proved him correct.

Len's daughter Mary lived just two blocks away in Chicago Ridge with her husband, Michael Bilder, and their five children. Len had grown fairly close to Mike despite their initial animosity. After their marriage in August of 1945, Mike and Mary moved into an upper apartment in the same building as Len and Maggie.

Sometimes on a Saturday afternoon Maggie and Mary would send Mike out after Len, who had slipped away to the local tavern to enjoy a boilermaker or two. Len would see Mike and say, "I know, I know, the women have sent you in here to come get me." Mike would always act surprised to see Len and respond, "No, I just dropped in for a drink myself." It was a ritual they both played well.

The two men would often share a few drinks and talk about many things including their combat experiences. If Mike had to get Len back a little quicker, he would start belting down shots of whiskey (as an experienced infantryman in Patton's Third Army and a very athletic guy, Mike had no trouble holding his liquor. He could out-drink Len with ease). Len would panic at the sight of his son-in-law drinking this way and quickly suggest they go home. That blissfully accomplished Mike's mission for the women.

Once Mike put a novelty whistle over the opening of the tail pipe of Len's car. Every time Len accelerated it let out a "wolf whistle" loud enough for everyone to hear. All the girls on the corner gave him a nasty look as if to say, "dirty old man." Poor Len almost died of embarrassment.

When Mike was elected Police Magistrate (Justice of the Peace) of Chicago Ridge in April of 1961, Len would often walk over to the evening hearings and sit in the back of the room proudly watching "Judge Bilder" as he rendered verdicts on speeding tickets and accused violators of local ordinances.

One day in the late spring of 1961, Len and Maggie were running errands. She was in a small retail store when he decided to run up to the second floor and see the local sawbones about a nagging sore throat. The heartless boob looked down Len's throat and said, "You've got throat cancer! Make an appointment tomorrow at Little Company and I'll take your tongue out." Len looked at him aghast and said, "Like hell I will."

Gene's wife was a nurse and set Len up with a physician she knew, but in 1961 there was little that could be done. Len's son-in-law, Claude Akins, offered to fund the latest cancer treatment at a clinic in California but again there was no real effective treatment, and Len and Maggie soon returned home. Len always despised anything he considered to be medical quackery.

He did submit to radiation treatments but they accomplished little other than to give him a leather-like neck. Maggie used a blender to liquefy his meals but he essentially gave up and went down hill rather rapidly. Just after New Year's Day in 1962 he went into a coma and was taken to Ingalls Hospital in Harvey. He developed pneumonia but unlike 1919, he did not recover. He died on January 6th without regaining consciousness.

The man who was confident his funeral would not have enough mourners to fill a single car would have been pleased. Mike had arranged for a police escort using squad cars from both Worth and Chicago Ridge while Father Jeffry had so many Carmelite priests concelebrating the funeral mass at Our Lady of the Ridge Church that it looked like a Cardinal was being buried. The church was packed with Len's children, their spouses, and a slew of grandchildren. There were former workmates from Prest-O-Lite and, of course, Al Slowey who was there to say good-bye to his lifelong friend and comrade in arms. Al lived until 1986.

Len was laid to rest in Holy Sepluchre Cemetery on one of the coldest January days on record. Maggie missed him greatly but followed the advice she had given to so many others in their times of trouble—"Press on, press on!" Maggie suffered a stroke in March of 1988 and passed away a few days later. Her burial beside her Len finally reunited the two sweethearts forever.

Acknowledgments

Many thanks are owed to many people. Despite an overwhelming schedule, Adriana Schroeder, the Command Historian for the Illinois National Guard, always found time for my requests. She made records, diaries, and countless bits of important details available. Also, thanks to First Sergeant Bill Lear, the Curator of the Illinois State War Museum at Camp Lincoln in Springfield, who made many photos available, as did Mary Manning the Reference Librarian at the Colonel Robert R. McCormick Research Center at the First Division Museum at Cantigny (Wheaton, IL).

Also, thanks to Gordon Blaker, the Curator and Director of the US Army Artillery Museum at Fort Sill, Oklahoma. To the members of the 2nd Battalion of the 122nd Field Artillery, Illinois National Guard, who took the time to explain in detail artillery tactics and methods.

Renowned Military Historian and personal friend Flint Whitlock who wrote the book's Foreword and Colonel Mark C. Jackson of the Army National Guard who currently serves as the Commander of Illinois' 33rd Infantry Brigade Combat Team (IBCT) for taking time to offer his gracious comments on my manuscript.

Authors Greg Jacobs, *Camp Grant*, Lt Col (US Army, Retired) John Votaw, *The American Expeditionary Forces in World War I*, and Thomas Hoff, *US Doughboy 1916–19*, for their kindness in assisting me with the numerous specifics about equipment, places, and circumstance that provide so much in making a story complete.

My daughter Jacqui Bilder, a graduate of DePaul University who specializes in sound and graphic design, for her composition of the book's maps. My son, Specialist James M. Bilder of the 33rd IBCT, who covered the precise details of land navigation and how the infantry uses it to coordinate strikes with their supporting artillery.

My sister, Marianne Grisolano, and her daughter Jennifer, both of whom have graduate degrees in writing, who completed the copyediting. Finally, my sincere thanks to my wife Bernie (Bernadette) who helps in any way she can, and who is always a constant source of inspiration.